Mr Wason ... I Think

For Leslie Murtim.

From one ecclesiastical oddity - - - -
To another, - - - - -
About another - - -

Mr Wason ...
I Think

by
Roy Tricker

Roy Tricker

Jan 95

With poems by the
Rev. Sandys Wason

Gracewing.

First Published in 1994
Gracewing
Fowler Wright Books
Southern Avenue, Leominster
Herefordshire HR6 0QF

Gracewing Books are distributed

In New Zealand by
Catholic Supplies Ltd
80 Adelaide Rd
Wellington
New Zealand

In Australia by
Charles Paine Pty
8 Ferris Street
North Parramatta
NSW 2151 Australia

In Canada by
Meakin & Assoc.
Unit 17, 81, Auriga Drive
Nepean
Ontario
KZE 7YS
Canada

In U.S.A. by
Morehouse Publishing
P.O. Box 1321
Harrisburg
PA 17105
U.S.A.

Printed and bound by The Cromwell Press, Melksham, Wiltshire

ISBN 085244 291 2

Contents

Foreword

The Catholic League was founded as an Anglican Society on 2nd July 1913. Its objectives are: fellowship amongst Catholics; the reunion of all Christians with Rome; the spread of the Catholic faith and the deepening of the spiritual life. Fr Sandys Wason, sometime Parish Priest of Cury with Gunwalloe in Cornwall was a pioneer priest of everything the League has stood for for over 80 years.

He was four years in the diaconate at Elmswell, Suffolk, because the Bishop of Ely, Alwyn Compton, refused to ordain him a priest so long as he insisted on using his Rosary. At Gunwalloe he was inhibited for prayer for the departed, and at Cury for the service of Benediction. He was wholly committed to the reunion of the Church of England with the Holy See of Peter and would have agreed with these words of Archbishop Nicholas Heath, Archbishop of York in 1555, who said: 'By the relinquishing and forsaking of the See of Rome, we must forsake and flee from all General Councils... We must forsake and flee from the unity of Christ's Church, and by leaping out of Peter's ship, hazard ourselves to be overwhelmed and drowned in the waters of sects and divisions.' Above all, Fr Wason was a man of prayer. His Breviary was always with him and he could be found reciting it at the pub, when he visited friends and even when he rode his bicycle! An acquaintance wrote: 'Whatever he may be doing, he will at some period of the day sink back into the Breviary, his fingers beginning automatically to fumble and probe into the pages of the ancient black book while he talks to you and grows more absent. I have never known him, however eager he might be about some other work, to forget the Office.' He best remembered Wason as the priest 'withdrawing into the secret world of the Holy Mass, unlocking a door which he alone seems able to enter, yet leaving it sufficiently open for us to see something of the light outside.'

The Mass certainly permeated the world outside. The story of Fr Wason and Fr Walke genuflecting absentmindedly towards the stage at a London theatre had a deep significance when Fr Wason said: 'Everything's Mass to me.'

Roy Tricker has done some excellent research. Though best known as a staunch preservationist of churches and an incurable ecclesiologist, he also has an encyclopaedic knowledge of Anglo-Catholic priests and their battles for the Catholic faith in the C of E. He was the obvious choice for writing this biography of Fr Wason. We include a commendation from the late Canon Miles Brown, who was to have been asked to write the foreword, but unfortunately died before the book went to press.

The story, published at the time of the 75th anniversary of Fr Wason's ejection from his living, could not appear at a more appropriate time as the League sails the uncharted waters of today's radically changed church, and it may give heart to priests and people experiencing 'the dark night of the soul'. May we renew our commitment to the League's objectives and take to heart those words attributed to John Keble:

What have we to expect? Anything.
What have we to hope for? Everything.
What have we to fear? Nothing.
For the battle is not ours, but God's.

Fr Philip T. Gray, B.A., S.S.C.
Priest Director of the Catholic League.
Vicar of Mendlesham, Suffolk

Introduction

'Mr Wason, I think'! retorted the Bishop of Truro to Fr. Bernard Walke, in response to his apology for a disturbance at his Institution to the parish of St. Hilary in 1912, when Fr. Wason, having taken exception to something said in the sermon, had marched towards the pulpit, waving a handker-chief which had previously covered his face as he sat dozing in the chancel stalls!

The Reverend Father Leighton Sandys Wason 'blazed a trail' (to quote Fr. Walke) wherever he went. He argued with, defied and sometimes outwitted Churchwardens, Archdeacons, Bishops, Disciplinary Courts and militant Protestants. Long before many of the most 'extreme' churches dared to even dream of doing so, he taught his people to honour Jesus Christ in the Blessed Sacrament by blessing them with the monstrance at the service of Benediction, he solemnly cast wreaths into the sea on All Souls Day, he venerated the Cross and celebrated the Mass of the Presanctified on Good Friday and he unashamedly used the Roman Missal in his Anglican churches. Church of England clergyman that he was, he never hid his detestation for the Reformation and the Book of Common Prayer, nor his vision of the Anglican Church as part of Catholic Christendom which looked to Rome for its final authority.

He wrote novels, poetry, religious pamphlets and some of the best Nonsense Verse of his day. One Bishop refused to ordain him Priest, another placed him under discipline and a third deprived him of his living. He saw his home ransacked, his worldly possessions thrown onto three horse-drawn wagons and was then physically ejected from his vicarage. After this he ran a London bookshop where he was rude to the customers, he lived in a Welsh council house, a Suffolk school caretaker's cottage, a little room at the end of an old York church and finally two rooms in the heart of London's Dockland.

He drew a mixed response from those who encountered him. His memory is still venerated by many in the English Church for his brave stand in defence of Benediction and other 'extreme' practices which many churches, thanks to people like him, now enjoy unmolested. Others see him as a Romanising heretic, unfaithful to his Oath of Canonical Obedience and a traitor to the Reformed Church. People admire his courage, his spirituality, his childlike humility, his poetry and writings – they are fascinated by his character, his wit, his eccentricity. One parishioner said 'He taught me the love of Our Lord'; another called him 'A bloody curse to his parish and his country'. Somebody with no religious axe to grind about him said 'Wason was a silly man ... I suppose his centre was his childish faith. Everything about him was rather childish. He never seems to have taken himself in hand or been taken in hand'.

Whatever one's feelings are about this controversial character, it is clear that this Faith, as he understood it, was so strong and uncompromising that no amount of ill-treatment or unpopularity could ever shake it, or make him shrink from what he believed to be his God-given vocation and ministry.

He would not approve of this booklet about him. He was a very private person, who spoke very little about himself. Of the many stories told about him he used to say, 'All lies! I don't know where people pick up these stories about me'.

I became fascinated by Fr. Wason thirty years ago and have learned a tremendous amount about him, but I am painfully aware that I never actually knew him personally – and that is my greatest handicap in this attempt to write something which is worthy of him. To compensate for my lack of this essential qualification, I have made the utmost use of a wealth of resources made available to me by people who have gone out of their way to help me, or whose writings have preserved precious insights and memories in print.

I would have never have been able to begin had not Fr. Peter Blagdon-Gamlen made his large collection of 'Wasonia' and a host of personal memories available to me. Further precious documents were shared with me by Fr. Michael Burgess, who made me welcome at his Rectory at Oughtrington. A major source of unpublished information has been the detailed records of Fr. Wason's ministry at Cury and Gunwalloe, collected by the late Mr. T. Ralph Nelson and the late Canon G. W. S. Harmer and made available to me by the Staff of the Cornwall Record Office at Truro.

I gladly acknowledge information gleaned from 'Twenty Years at St. Hilary', by Bernard Walke, also 'The Road was Free', 'The Call of Cornwall' and an article in the Cornish Review entitled 'The Perpetual Curate of Cury-with-Gunwalloe' – all by Frank Baker. Mr. Alex Roberts, Secretary of the Protestant Truth Society has graciously provided me with copies of relevant articles from the 'Churchman's Magazine' and has kindly allowed me to quote from them.

What a joy it has been to meet Mr. Stanley Tonkin of Mullion, Miss Mary Thorold of Welwyn Garden City and Mrs. F. Brett of Needham Market, who actually knew Fr. Wason and were delighted to share with me their vivid memories of him, also to read letters written to other people some years ago containing more personal recollections.

The Rev'd Dr. Peter Long, the present parish priest of Cury-with-Gunwalloe, made me welcome in his benefice, showed me everything that I needed to see and shared his own considerable knowledge with me. Then there are the many folk, including Ricci and Katrin Howkins, Roger Tomlinson, Ian Battersby, David Wilderspin, Fr. Christopher Colven, Dorothy Storry, and others who deserve my thanks.

My wife, Jennifer, has laboriously scrutinised my original draft and has saved me much embarrassment by correcting errors of typing and punctuation. Frs. Peter Blagdon-Gamlen, Peter Long, Mr. Dennis Castey and Canon H. Miles Brown have also read the typescript and given helpful advice. I have also been greatly encouraged, cajoled and nagged, by Fr. Philip Gray, Vicar of Mendlesham and Priest Director of the Catholic League, who was determined that a book about Fr. Wason should be written and that I should have the privilege and immense joy of researching and writing it.

Roy Tricker,
Ipswich.

Commendation by the late Canon Miles Brown

A sympathetic and proportional account of a man of character whom one cannot ignore, even if his standpoint is not shared. A considerable amount of research has obviously gone into this story and I for one am grateful for the unveiling of the early years, which have always been vague to me.

Wason's time in Cornwall coincided with a growing frustration with the Church of England as it was, and the Anglo-Catholic movement attracted many writers, authors and actors to its ranks. This attraction blossomed in the great Congresses just after Wason's time, and it is interesting to read of the number of people like Compton Mackenzie etc. who gravitated to Cury and to St Hilary at this time. One rather suspects what with many it was not only a desire to share in a worship more satisfying than the usual dull, state-controlled C of E, but also the glamour of Rome without the discipline that Church would exact.

This work vividly recalls a bygone age when the Anglican clergy were individuals and could become eccentrics or develop their gifts and scholarship. Nowadays the colleges are producing ordinands who know or care nothing about their own church's history or theology and who are caught up in the latest idea, and in their parishes swamped with paper and administration. I say nothing about women 'priests' which have the responsibility for negating any claim the Church of England had to be part of the One Holy Catholic Church. It is good to be reminded of those who have worked in obscure parts of the vineyard doing what they thought best for their people without seeking promotion or prominence, even if their conception of their duty seems odd to us.

Part One

The Pre-Cury Years

Father Wason casually passed to his friend and fellow-author Frank Baker one day the following details about himself, scribbled upon a piece of paper which he had torn out of an old notebook:-

'Born, Dec. 31st 1867; Baptized, May 9th 1868; Mother died, 1880; Father died, 1883; Confirmation 1884; Westminster School 1881–84; Paris – Hanover 1884; Christ Church Oxford, 1889–93; Deacon, 23rd December 1894; Priest, 25th September 1898.' This appears to be the only evidence proffered by the man himself about his early life. Hence we know very little about his family and next to nothing about his childhood and adolescence, or of the people, places or circumstances which in his formative years were to mould his character and beliefs.

Leighton Sandys Wason entered this world on the last day of the year 1867, at Montague Square, London, although his birth was not registered (at Marylebone) until the second quarter of 1868. His father was Rigby Melvill Wason, who was born in Lancashire in 1840 and studied Law at Cambridge, graduating as an Ll.B. in 1864 and qualifying as a Solicitor in 1867. His office was at 6 South Square, Grays Inn. He married in 1865 Hannah Urquhart and Leighton Sandys was their only child. His paternal grandfather was the Rev'd John James Wason, Vicar of Sheepscombe Gloucestershire and resident for a time in the St. Michael's District of Bristol, who married Charlotte, daughter of Col. William Sandys of Lanarth, which explains Fr. Wason's second Christian name. This made him a descendant of Edwin

3

Sandys, Archbishop of York, who died in 1588. It is interesting that this prelate, who is described as one who did his
utmost to further the principles of the English Reformation,
was a keen opponent of Romish practices and even had
personal leanings towards Puritan ideals, should be com-
memorated in Southwell Minster by a splendid alabaster
monument, showing his recumbent effigy vested in an alb and
chasuble – his wife and eight children kneeling beneath!

It seems that Fr. Wason much preferred his second
Christian name and he rarely used the first. He always signed
'Sandys Wason,' or 'S.W.' and his close friends always knew
him as Sandys. Only when signing the Marriage Registers in
his parishes did he use both names, as the Law required.

What must have had a devastating effect upon the young
Sandys was the early death of his parents. Hannah died, aged
42, at Herne Bay on September 18th 1880 (when her son was
twelve years old) and Rigby Melvill died in New York on June
26th 1883. It appears that the orphaned teenager's upbringing
was entrusted to his aunts and cousins – the Biddulph family.
He attended Westminster School from 1881–4, leaving at the
age of 16 for what he describes as 'Paris-Hanover'. His
College Register states that he spent some time serving in the
'Artillery', before going up to Christ Church Oxford in 1889
at the rather late age of 21.

Sandys' undergraduate years at Oxford were greatly to
influence his thought and personality, and to nourish and
develop his many talents. Here he would have met people who
had known Dr. Pusey and the early pioneers of the Catholic
Revival, which had been launched 55 years before at this very
university and which, with the 'Second Generation' of Anglo-
Catholics, had become more 'advanced' in its thinking and
expression – the more extreme amongst its adherents taking
the Papalist viewpoint, which unashamedly coupled the
doctrine and practice of the Church of England with that of
the Holy See.

Here also Sandys could be himself – learning to be his own
man, to plough his own very distinctive furrow in the world
and to detach himself from the 'rat-race' – all characteristics
which marked him out in later life as a very unique and
singular personality. Compton Mackenzie wrote that he had

arrived at Oxford with the reputation of having married a widow with 14 children — 'but being Wason he carried off this ridiculous legend with as much dignity as in later years he carried off episcopal visitations and archidiaconal admonishments'.

It was during his Oxford days that his literary talent began to flourish. In 1891 he founded, with his fellow undergraduates Herbert Grierson (later Sir Herbert, the literary scholar) and John Phillimore (the great Classical scholar), and edited, a periodical called 'The Spirit Lamp', which published contributions by people such as Oscar Wilde and Max Beerbohm. Compton Mackenzie said of this journal of wit, wisdom and verse (its strange title referring to a method of heating water) that 'the 1890s and all that they stood for' were included in it and it 'attacked decadence almost before it appeared'. Wason invited Lewis Carroll (C. L. Dodgson — later the Rev'd, but in Deacon's Orders to the end of his life) to contribute, but received the terse printed reply 'Mr. Dodgson does not contribute to the Press' — to which Wason countered 'The Editors regret that they cannot make use of the enclosed communication'. Dodgson was Curator of the Common Room at Christ Church until 1892 and lived in rooms there for several more years and so Wason was probably in contact with him there. Both became skilful writers of nonsense verse. We see in the undergraduate Sandys Wason an emerging literary 'aesthete', foreshadowing the type of university aesthetic talent and lifestyle later enjoyed by John Betjeman and his contemporaries at Oxford.

We know nothing Wason's early spiritual development, nothing of who or what fostered his vocation to the priesthood, or who planted and kindled in him the uncompromising Papalism which was to be the mainstay of his Christianity and his ministry. The Oxford of the '80s and '90s must have played its part, because he left there for Ely Theological College to train for a year before Ordination.

He was made Deacon on December 23rd 1894 by Bishop Alwyne Compton of Ely and served his title at the Suffolk village church of St. John the Divine at Elmswell, under Fr. James Hipwell who between 1893–1908 made Elmswell one of Suffolk's few village Catholic centres. Shortly after his departure it was placed very firmly in Evangelical hands!

The Elmswell Service Register records on Christmas Day 1894 'The Rev'd L. S. Wason came' and it seems that an important part of his ministry there was with the Elmswell children. He was responsible for the 'Catechising' or the 'Children's Service' which took place every Sunday at 2.45 p.m. During Lent 1896 he held a Children's Service each Friday − the titles of his talks being 'Little Daisies', 'Forget-me-Nots', 'Little Doctors', and 'Little Gardeners'! Another curate, the Rev'd A. Collier, had joined in 1895 and Wason's last mention in the Register was in September 1896.

It must have been frustrating to his parish priest and even more so to himself, that for some reason Bishop Compton refused to Priest him and he had to remain in Deacon's Orders throughout his time there. It is said that this was because he insisted upon using the Rosary as part of his private devotions.

In 1897 he moved to spend a year as curate in the vast parish of St. Andrew's Plaistow, whose mighty brick church (a masterpiece of James Brooks) was a caring Catholic centre near where Essex and London joined. It was whilst he was here that Bishop John Festing of St. Albans priested him in 1898 and he was able to offer the first of thousands of Masses, which he regarded as his premier duty throughout his life.

In 1899 he became curate at St. Michael's, Mark Street, Shoreditch − another splendid Brooks church, less than 10 minutes walk from Liverpool Street Station. Though closed in 1964, this fine church (which from its birth in 1864 was such a stronghold of the Catholic Revival) still stands, although its adjoining Convent and Hospital have gone. During Fr. Wason's time there, St. Michael's was one of the most 'extreme' churches in London and had fallen foul of diocesan 'authority'. Bishop Creighton had forbidden certain 'goings on' there, but to no avail and even Bishop Winnington Ingram, who often went out of his way to accommodate the Catholic Movement in his diocese, felt that he must be seen to be taking action here. Despite personal pleading by Lord Halifax not to do so, the Bishop, after a pastoral remonstration and an Episcopal Monition had been issued and ignored, served a Prosecution in 1903 'in consequence of the public use in the church of services and devotions other than those contained in the authorised service books, not only without the sanction of the Bishop, but in defiance of his directions to refrain from using them'.

The Vicar, Fr. Herbert M. M. Evans (who came there in 1891 from the parish of Coveney, near Ely) promptly resigned and made his submission to the Church of Rome, together with one of his curates and several of the congregation. It is said that the departure was dramatic – clergy and congregation walking out of the church and marching in procession up the road to make their submission. Fr. Wason's figure however remained in the pulpit, loudly reciting the Rosary, with the remnant that had also remained. Although it was feared that a new Vicar of Protestant persuasion would be put in, a hardworking Anglo-Catholic (Fr. Henry Ross, from St. Bartholomew's Brighton) was wisely appointed and many of the congregation returned. Fr. Wason remained for a further year, before leaving for the countryside of far Cornwall – to his first and only living.

Perpetual Curate of Cury-with-Gunwalloe

In 1905, Sandys Wason arrived in the Duchy of Cornwall and the Diocese of Truro – that far south-western corner of England which is still very much an entity in itself and which could be described as being 'in' England, but not quite 'of' it! This wild county of lonely villages with grey granite churches, dedicated to the many Celtic saints who planted the Faith there, has nourished many an eccentric, not least amongst its clergy. It has also become a seed-bed of the Catholic Revival in the Church of England, thanks in no small part to people like Fr. Wason, who were prepared to make a firm stand by their principles and were made to suffer for so doing.

The small parishes of Cury and Gunwalloe are situated on the western side of the Lizard Peninsula, within a few miles of England's most southerly point. The A3083 passes through Cury parish and the little settlement known as Cury Cross Lanes; the church and vicarage are in Cury village, about a mile to the west. The pretty pinnacled tower of the Church of St. Corentin rises above the scattered cottages and the large Methodist Church. Here we may admire the 15th century architecture of the north aisle and the attractive mixture of rooflines of the nave, porch and transept on the south side as we make for the splendid and greening Norman doorway, which reminds us that people have worshipped here for 900 years. From the door are pleasant views across to Mullion. A delightful and readable 'Pilgrim's Guide' tells us the church's history and points us to its treasures, so suffice it to say that today's pilgrim will find a cherished and cared-for church of character, which feels like Holy Ground.

Restorers of 1873 gave it the present unusual roofs, with their pendants, also the benches and pulpit (the latter now in the south-west corner) and a sensitive re-ordering of 1979 cleared the chancel of clutter and installed a new High Altar, although the framed (1873) porcelain tablets with the Lord's Prayer, Creed and Commandments are still on the east wall and the Victorian reredos of stone quatrefoils which Wason would have seen at close quarters many times is now hidden by a curtain. The glass in the east window (showing Christ the King, flanked by Our Lady and St. John) had just been inserted when he arrived at Cury. It was presented by the Hon Sir John Langdon Bonython of Adelaide in September 1904. The two windows in the Lady Chapel were given by the same family in 1922 and 1939. Members of this family had owned Bonython Manor (just east of the A3083) where a stable has been converted into a small Private Chapel (consecrated in 1978 and used as a Mission Church) through the efforts of Fr. F. W. Marshall, who was Vicar of Cury and Gunwalloe from 1965–74. It is to this humble and atmospheric little Chapel that we must come to see the choir stalls from Cury Church and the High Altar which Wason used and into which he set an altar-stone of figured marble.

Standing in Cury's quaint interior, we see so much that Wason saw when he was its priest. He baptised youngsters in the Norman font; he used the little sacristy in part of the south transept, behind the benches which are now the stalls for members of the Fraternity of Knights of St. Corentin – a group of people who have links with Cury, but live outside the United Kingdom and are linked together by a simple Rule of Life. He would have seen the two sets of rood-loft stairs (and maybe dreamed of restoring the screen, as has been done at Mullion) and the strange little passage with its low-side window at the junction of transept and chancel. It was he who removed the organ from the east end of the north aisle and set up the Lady Chapel there, revealing again the eastern window with the stonecarving in its rere-arch. He would surely approve of the Continental-looking statue of Our Lady, and of the tabernacle on the altar here, also the super-frontal on the High Altar, asking the prayers of the church's Patron Saint.

Travelling westwards from the church, after about a quarter of a mile we reach the Old Vicarage, where Wason lived, on our left — having in fact just crossed over into the parish of Gunwalloe. The white-painted house is compact and not large as parsonage houses go, but its exterior has the unmistakable character of a vicarage. The stables which Wason used are still there, with their original floors and courtyard of cobblestones. To the south, the sloping and terraced lawns sweep down and there is a splendid vista to Mullion over open country. During Wason's time there was a tennis court on the first terrace. He enjoyed playing tennis and there is a photograph of him with Fr. Walke, ready to play, dressed in a blazer, white slacks, clerical collar and, of course, his biretta! On the left upon entering the house is the 'Murder Room', where, in Sir Arthur Conan Doyle's 'The Adventure of The Devil's Foot', a body was found seated beside a centre table, his face turned towards the window.

Continuing westwards along the lane, we pass the house called 'Pendragon', where lived Charles Turley Smith — author, tutor, but best known as the book reviewer and critic for 'Punch' magazine. He attracted around him many of the most eminent literary figures of the day including, in addition to Conan Doyle, James Barrie and A. A. Milne. He was a friend of Fr. Wason during his time here, although he did not share his 'extreme' brand of churchmanship and often worshipped at nearby St. Mawgan and Mullion churches. He was a major figure in the development of Mullion Golf Course, which we soon reach, and across which a footpath takes us directly to Gunwalloe Church. The founder of the Golf Course (in 1895) — one William Sich — was Church-warden of Gunwalloe, but resigned in protest at Fr. Wason's 'excessive rituals'. The path across the Golf Course was the one which Wason always took to church, passing on weekdays golfers out for their sport and recreation (Sunday play was successfully resisted by Messrs Sich and Turley Smith until the 1930s). Occasionally he would find some of these people searching for their lost golf-balls in and around Gunwalloe churchyard and would always assume that they were on their way to the service and would say 'Come along now, Mass in five minutes. This way!'

If we stay on the lane, rather than taking the path across the Golf Course, we soon descend into Poldhu Cove, on the other side of which rises the former Poldhu Hotel, in the parish of Mullion. During Wason's time, this palatial pile was dwarfed by the four massive pylons of Marconi's transmission station, where the first radio transmission was made to Newfoundland in 1901. On the Golf Course side of Poldhu Cove is a cottage called Craigabella, where Holmes and Watson are described as staying in 'The Devil's Foot'.

Approaching Gunwalloe by footpath (either Wason's way over the Golf Links, or by the footpath from Poldhu), the journey and the views are unforgettable, as we look across dramatic coastal scenery. The setting of the church in its cove and only yards from the beach is surely one of the most spectacular settings for an English church. Approaching by road from Helston, we take a lane from the A3083 which winds over the hills and then down to the small cluster of houses which is Gunwalloe village, passing on our right the pretty white-painted thatched cottage (beside the Mission Room, with its gable cross) where Sir Compton Mackenzie resided. A signpost announces that the church is a further 1½ miles and we finally reach the idyllic little cove in which it is set, with views to the golf links and the Poldhu Hotel, and sands stretching round to the rocks beneath the knoll into which the Church of St. Winwalloe is built. We can imagine the All Souls Day procession to these rocks, upon which priest and servers stood precariously to cast the wreath into the sea.

What a fascinating character this seaside church − its body typically Cornish, with its three uniform roof-lines and punctuated by neat two and three-light windows. It is set in a sloping, windswept churchyard, which rises to the curious squat and detached bell-house (others may be seen at Feock, Gwennap and elsewhere in Cornwall), built into the hillside. Inside, the church is homely, atmospheric and colourful − and visitors are made to feel very much expected and welcome here. The attractive 'Pilgrim's Guide' tells us about St. Winwalloe, of J. D. Sedding's restoration of the church in 1871, and of the treasures ancient and modern to be enjoyed here. The crystals sparkle in the 14th century granite arcades. Of granite also is the High Altar, designed by Sir Ninian Comper and given by Fr. Wason in memory of his mother. The north chapel altar came from the Mission Room and the tabernacle here was almost certainly one which Wason used; it was found in the Vicarage stables and was restored to its rightful purpose in 1980.

Wason would approve of the benches, carved by Herbert Read of Exeter, and the screens which divide the side chapels from the chancel − erected after his time here. The east window, showing Our Lord with blood pouring from his Sacred Heart into a chalice (in memory of a person who died in 1921) would have pleased him greatly! It must be acknowledged that Fr. Wason's successor, the Rev'd William Valentine Wagner (here from 1920−36 and later Vicar of Mylor, then of Paul, in this diocese) − even if he was a moderate Evangelical, trained at Ridley Hall Cambridge and appointed to counteract his predecessor's papalism − initiated some very tasteful and beautiful improvements in Gunwalloe Church.

Into this fascinating corner of England, enthusiastic and fired by life at one of Inner London's most 'extreme' churches, came Sandys Wason in 1905 as Perpetual Curate of Cury-with-Gunwalloe. A Perpetual Curate was licensed by the Bishop without any form of Institution or Induction, upon the nomination of a Lay Rector who, in this case, was Captain Rogers the Squire of Penrose, in the village of Porthlevan, some miles further west, but whose land holdings extended to the cliffs around Gunwalloe church. Porthlevan was itself a centre of the Anglo-Catholic tradition. Rogers supported the Catholic Movement in the Church of England and knew its London strongholds, including St. Michael's Shoreditch. The frail and aged Bishop John Gott of Truro (who died the following year) advised the 38 year old priest embarking upon his first curé to be cautious and patient with his people, many of whom were Nonconformists. The total population of the benefice at that time was about 300 souls, who had the choice of two Parish Churches, a Mission Room and four Nonconformist Chapels.

Wason's predecessor was the Rev'd Joseph Chambers, who

had been there since 1878, had grown old and died there. 'Passon Chambers' was remembered as somebody who simply 'sat in his study and waited for something to do', and so his successor inherited an isolated and neglected vicarage, two neglected churches and two villages where most of the Christian life centred around the Methodist Chapels. John Wesley had preached in the area in 1762 and by Wason's time Methodism of a very earnest and ultra-Protestant type had been firmly established as the Divine Alternative to the Established Church. Wason and Wesley would have probably enjoyed each other's company, especially as Wesley was known in his early days to have used a form of the Rosary as a spiritual exercise, to have gone to Communion daily and had always insisted that his followers presented themselves at the altar of their parish church to receive the Sacrament. But Cornish Methodism was very militant, especially in villages where the Established Church (which enjoyed being 'Established' and resisted change) had gone to sleep and Nonconformity had taken the upper hand.

Had Fr. Wason heeded his Bishop's advice, he may well have had considerable success, but winning people over slowly by gentle and gradual change and maybe just a little compromise was not in his nature and from the first week of his ministry there, Cury and Gunwalloe were to 'enjoy' full Catholic privileges and undiluted Papalism whether they liked it or not! There was no question of argument, discussion or an alternative opinion. The services on his first Sunday were Holy Communion at 8 a.m., Devotions and Sermon at 11 a.m. and Vespers and Sermon at 6 p.m. From the pulpit he announced that from henceforth there would be daily Mass at 8 a.m., with Sung Mass at 11 a.m. and Devotions at 6 p.m. on Sundays, and that the Bishop of Lebombo would be singing the Mass on the following Sunday. And all this to a congregation seated in good erastian tradition, with the farmers and the Squire's party occupying the front pews and the lesser mortals respectfully at the back, all of whom had been brought up upon a diet consisting mostly of Morning Prayer and Sermon.

Their new priest made an initial impression upon some of the locals though, and word soon got around that 'Passon' was a strange fellow 'but can't he preach'! Although not a respecter of persons, he did have a great love for the poor and needy and it was the humble labouring folk who came to church, where they were welcomed and were taught the Faith – and several remained Wason's loyal supporters. Having transformed the services, taking the content of most of them from the Roman Missal rather than from the Book of Common Prayer (his detestation for which he never hid, regarding it as totally heretical and the Reformation as a sacreligious disaster), he then rubbed salt into the wounds of his 'aggrieved parishioners' at his first Easter Vestry Meeting. Here he shocked everybody by appointing as his Vicar's Warden a farm labourer called Alfred Thomas, in place of the Squire (Major Lee of Bochym Manor) who had held the position for years. The leading lights of the parish appointed as People's Warden a butcher named Bowden in the hope that he would 'keep Passon in his place' and would curb his popish activities. Mr. Bowden duly made his presence felt shortly afterwards when Wason turned his attention towards beautifying the church and was determined to have the organ out of the east end of the north aisle where it blocked up what should rightly be the Lady Chapel. About this time, Captain and Mrs. Rogers (the Patrons) gave a plaster statue of the Virgin and Child and Wason placed crucifixes on the altar and above the pulpit. One person wrote that as each innovation arrived, Fr. Wason 'with his inscrutable smile' taught the people from the pulpit 'what it was all about'. Mr. Churchwarden Bowden however wrote to the Bishop, who summoned Wason to see him, but he returned having received his Lordship's blessing and a gentle warning not to antagonise the Squire.

About the same time as Fr. Wason arrived at Cury, his old friend whom he had known in his London days, Fr. Bernard Walke, arrived as Curate-in-Charge of Polruan, near Fowey, where he was to remain until the start of his own very eventful ministry at St. Hilary in 1912. Fr. Walke had a young parishioner at Polruan called Thomas Ralph Nelson, who needed employment and a start in life, so he sent him to Cury to live at the vicarage and to help Fr. Wason in his house, garden and churches. It is to this Ralph Nelson that we owe many of the details of Fr. Wason's ministry in Cornwall. He kept a scrapbook with notes and pictures of his time there, also another scrapbook in which Wason himself had preserved a multitude of newspaper cuttings, and in later years Ralph wrote a short and very readable autobiography. These documents are now in the care of the Cornwall Record Office. Ralph was devoted to Fr. Wason and writes 'He taught me the love of Our Lord'.

Wason's introduction to Gunwalloe was equally eventful. Here was a stretch of coastline with treacherous rocks upon which many ships had met undignified ends – their hulls being smashed up by the rocks, their crews battered to death or drowned and their contents plundered by wreckers. Wrecking was a custom in Cornish coastal villages. Word came that a ship was aground or wrecked and the locals were there to remove everything of value that they could get their hands upon, be it cargo, furniture or the personal possessions of the ill-fated crew. Like another Cornish priest – the Rev'd R. S. Hawker of Morwenstow – Wason detested this custom. He preached against it from Gunwalloe's pulpit to sturdy Cornishmen and, on November 2nd 1905, his first All Souls Day in the parish, he began the custom of celebrating a sung Requiem Mass in the church, followed by a solemn procession to the nearby rocks, where he threw a wreath of flowers into the sea in memory of all who had drowned on that stretch of coastline that year and previous years. A series of postcards was produced of this ceremony during later years, showing the procession along the sands and Wason, in cope and biretta, attended by crucifer, thurifer, boat-boy and acolytes and backed by his congregation (including godly-looking ladies in large Edwardian hats), standing precariously upon the rocks and solemnly casting the wreath of 'immortelles' into the sea, symbolising the people's prayers for those who had perished in it. One year this ceremony was attended by Wason's bull-terrier, who immediately dashed into the water, swam out and faithfully retrieved the wreath for his master! The All Souls-tide ceremony of course attracted much opposition, until the sinking of the 'Titanic' in 1912 – the first sad news of which was received at the Radio Station at Poldhu. After this it took on a new and very real meaning and even the most hardened opponent could not (or dared not) object to it as just another piece of eccentric superstition.

It was the custom of the locals to place the bodies of drowned seamen in the detached tower, where the police would go to view them for inquests. This did not please Wason, who caused a little trouble around 1908 when he and Ralph Nelson removed one such body, laid the person out properly, wrapped him in a sheet and placed him in the church, where appropriate prayers were said. The police visited the tower and found the body gone, and there was a little explaining to be done.

Gunwalloe's Burial Register records the interment of several such seamen. In 1915 Fr. Wason noted the burial of 'about 46, found drowned at Church Cove and Fishing Cove, from the "London Trader" '. Occasionally Fr. Scholefield of Mullion officiated at Burial Services, including that in 1916 for 'four men unknown in one grave', found drowned and thought to be from the wreck of the 'SS Heidrien' from Norway. It is interesting that the Norwegian Government is now planning to erect a memorial to these people.

Shortly after Wason's arrival, William Sich, who was also the Parish Chairman, and the other Gunwalloe Churchwarden, resigned and there was a stormy Easter Vestry Meeting. Wason chose as his Warden a gentle and retiring farmer called John Freeman, who was dominated by his two sisters but was kind to his labourers. The sisters and their maid, Annie Pascoe, supported Wason however and made vestments and altar cloths for him. During the First World War he was succeeded by Ralph Nelson as Vicar's Warden.

Gunwalloe's charming church was crying out to be made more beautiful and devotional and Wason felt that J. D. Sedding's rather heavy-handed restoration of 1869–71 had spoiled it somewhat. He replaced the wooden High Altar with one of granite at his own expense as a memorial to his mother and he had plans drawn up and displayed for a new oak screen, which caused one of the former Churchwardens to send a letter of protest to the Bishop, who prevented its erection. The altar (which had of course been put in without a faculty) was allowed to remain – mainly because nobody knew quite how to go about getting the faculty for its removal.

Several years later the artist, Sir Alfred Munnings, during a visit to St. Hilary, came down with Bernard Walke to visit Wason. Walke and Wason agreed that the Victorian varnished pitch-pine benches, the 'hideous pulpit' and the wooden vestry enclosure did not fit the primitive character of the church and resolved to get rid of them and purchase rush-seated chairs. Early one morning the two priests and the rather apprehensive Munnings used the grave-diggers' tools stored in the tower to dismantle the offending furnishings. Munnings wrote that 'growing bolder, with Walke, I heaved and sweated in earnest – clearing one pew after another, while Wason walked up and down the aisle, chanting from some holy text'. Wason later sold the pews to some large coastal tea-room and made enough money from the sale to purchase the chairs needed to replace them.

One of the former Churchwardens was Mr. Ranson, who owned Gunwalloe's only Hotel and Public House. He hated his new Vicar and called him 'A bloody curse to his parish and country'! The new People's Warden was Mr. John Williams, whose wife ran the Village Shop. Williams said that although he didn't 'altogether hold with Passon's views' he was a 'good payer' and patronised the shop. He was also happy to earn a little extra pin-money by tidying the vicarage garden once a week. Their little son, Leslie, was a cripple, but Wason spent time with the lad and taught him to serve at the altar, which he did on the occasions when he was well enough to walk. Ralph Nelson records that Mr. Williams proudly told people that his son 'do looking something purty in that gown thing and lacy cotta and old Passon has our boy up to the vicarage to eat his pasty and gives 'un teay when he goes to school, up to Cury'!

Another Gunwalloe character was Sam Bray, the organist, who not only played loudly but also sang loudly, to such an extent that poor Wason, who had absolutely no ear for music anyhow, offered to supply cotton-wool for those who could not bear the noise, and often wore it himself.

Shortly after Wason's arrival in Cornwall, Compton Mackenzie and Faith his wife came to live for a year at the vicarage as paying guests, and it was during this time that the greater part of his first novel 'The Passionate Elopement' was

written. Wason first encountered the adolescent Mackenzie at
Alton Abbey when he was still a Deacon and he provided the
ideal spiritual guide for the teenager, introducing him to the
Vicar of nearby Wield. It seems that Fr. Wason was then
taking a great interest in the early development of Alton
Abbey, founded as a mission to sailors and then in its first
corrugated-iron buildings, although Peter F. Anson informs
us that he was infuriated that the Brethren referred to
breakfast and afternoon tea as 'tiffin' and was shocked that
they used an Anglican Monastic Diurnal rather than the
Roman Breviarium Monasticum.

Whilst Mackenzie enjoyed playing two-handed bridge with
Wason most evenings at Cury, poor Faith was not very
church-minded and took exception to the fact that Wason
automatically expected her to act as the housekeeper. It is said
that she 'escaped' for a couple of months and returned, not to
the vicarage, but to the little white thatched cottage (called
Toy Cottage) which her husband had by then managed to
acquire in Gunwalloe. On Fr. Walke's recommendation,
Mackenzie was licensed as a Lay Reader in 1908 and began a
Sunday School, which he ran strictly 'on his own lines',
preferring to teach the children by taking them for long walks
and telling them morality stories about the birds, trees and
natural things that they encountered, rather than teaching
them the Catechism. Within a few weeks he had 23 scholars,
much to the annoyance of the local Methodists.

Compton Mackenzie wrote a trilogy of novels, entitled
'The Altar Steps', 'Parson's Progress' and 'The Heavenly
Ladder' in which the character of Father Oliver Dorward is
based upon Fr. Wason.

Fr. Nicolo Bernard Walke was Fr. Wason's very dear friend
and ally in his Cornish days. He was Curate-in Charge of
Polruan from 1905 until he became Vicar of St. Hilary in
1912. He too was a dedicated Anglo-Catholic in the Papalist
tradition, who taught the Faith to his Cornish folk with
considerable success. Annie, his wife, was a talented artist and
she and her friends (many of them artists of national repute)
transformed St. Hilary Church into a colourful and
devotional shrine. St. Hilary became known throughout the
country through its plays, written by Fr. Walke, which were

broadcast nationwide by the BBC. Walke was also known for the Children's Home which he founded at St. Hilary, called the 'Jolly Tinners', for the famous people from the world of art and literature who came to stay with him, and for the horrendous persecution which he suffered, culminating in 1932 when he saw so many of the objects of beauty in his lovely church smashed to pieces by an organised gang of 'protesters', armed with hammers and pickaxes but acting, so we are told, within the Law.

Fr. Walke knew and understood Wason as well as anybody and his own book 'Twenty Years at St. Hilary' gives us wonderful glimpses into the character of his old friend who, by 1912, seems to have achieved enough fame for St. Hilary locals to remark as the procession made its way up the church at Walke's Institution – 'There's old Wason over to Cury. He's a proper old Roman Catholic they do say. Can'ee see'm my dear? The one wearing a hat like a tea-cosy'. Wason was seated in the choir-stalls throughout the service, blissfully ignoring everything and engaged in saying his Rosary. It appears that he nodded off to sleep over this, having placed a handkerchief over his face, until the Bishop in his sermon began warning against 'extreme practices', whereupon Wason woke up, stood up and made for the pulpit. Fr. Walke had to physically place him back in his stall, waving his handkerchief and protesting 'You must not allow these things, Ber, to be said in your church'.

There were other Catholic parishes in the Kerrier Rural Deanery during Fr. Wason's time as a member of its chapter. From 1909–1918 his neighbour to the north-west at St. Mawgan in Meneage was the Rev'd Algernon Thorold, whose daughter Mary remembers him with great affection and speaks of him as 'one of my first boy-friends'. Clearly Wason made a lasting impression upon this young lady (who was only ten when her family left for the parish of Altarnun) on his many visits to see her father, who had previously been on the staff of Truro Cathedral. Evidently when he was due to leave the cathedral for St. Mawgan, one of the Canons warned Mrs. Thorold to keep her husband away from 'the pernicious influence of Fr. Wason'.

Fr. Thorold was not the extreme uncompromising papalist

that Fr. Wason was, but the two priests were great friends. Fr. Wason throughout his life was never the tidiest of people and Mary's brother Michael (later Vicar of All Souls Brighton) enjoyed going over to Cury and Gunwalloe to tidy up their churches, where Wason's vestments, books, etc., were always in a mess. Mary also clearly remembers that her father would never invite Wason to celebrate at St. Mawgan because he regarded him as rather slovenly when conducting services and feared that clearing up the mess after him would be a major operation! Nevertheless, Wason would cycle over to St. Mawgan vicarage and Mary still has visions of him on his bicycle, oblivious of the world around him, holding up his Breviary with one hand, deep in his Office. Once when it was her birthday, he brought over a bunch of cornflowers for her. A feature of Kerrier Deanery life was the lunches for the clergy, when they would meet together for study and discussion and then have lunch, each taking his turn to be the host. Fr. Wason took his full part in this and when one was held at Cury, there was a bottle of Communion wine on the lunch table.

When Dr. Thorold was due to leave St. Mawgan, it was planned that the parish should be united with St. Martin-in-Meneage, whose low-church Rector, the Rev'd William Reeder, arranged to visit Fr. Thorold to discuss and to see his additional charge. Wason was determined to be in on this interview and eagerly suggested to his friend that they should both be sure to wear their birettas in order to shock the Protestant Mr. Reeder!

The bearded and scholarly Fr. J. H. Scholefield, Vicar of Mullion, and Fr. Wason's neighbour to the south, was also an Anglo-Catholic and was especially kind and hospitable to him after the tragic happenings of 1919.

Wason into Battle

Sandys Wason had a very single-minded (some may prefer 'narrow-minded') attitude to his work and vocation. He saw himself as a priest of the Catholic Church, of which the Church of England was a very small part, and to him the final authority for what went on in the Catholic Church must be the Pope and the Holy See. He saw this as perfectly logical and straight-forward and with him there was no need for compromise, half-measures or any watering-down of his position. To him if you were an Anglican then you were a Catholic and you held the Catholic Faith – undiluted and in all its fullness. His duty as a priest was to teach the Faith and to administer the sacraments, as Holy Church directed. Many priests who embraced the principles of the Catholic Revival rejoiced in the Church of England as an entity in itself – Catholic but Reformed, with a Prayer Book which is basically and in essence Catholic and sacramental, and a doctrine which is free from all the 'additions and errors' which Rome has chosen to add over the years. This was not Wason's catholicism; he had no time for the Book of Common Prayer, saw the English Reformation as a tragedy and regarded the goal of the Ecclesia Anglicana as eventual reunion with the Holy See.

The 38 year old priest arrived from one of London's most extreme papalist churches, where there had been battles with Bishops and Protestant agitators and where many of the congregation had already given up with the Church of England and had made their submission to Rome. Now at last he had a living of his own, where he was the Parish Priest – where he could do something in his own right and could make his churches and parishes 'centres of the Faith'. No wonder his parishioners were surprised, shocked and sometimes hostile. Most of them were ardent Methodists and Cury's Squire and church-folk knew nothing and wanted nothing other than the sleepy erastian type of 'churchianity' of the Church of England 'by Law Established'. Maybe a more moderate form of catholicism, gradually and gently introduced, may have won many more of them over — but that just wasn't in Wason's nature. It was not that he did not love the people — rather it was his burning desire that they should enjoy the fullness of the Faith from the beginning.

The Cury Squire disliked him not least for replacing him with a labourer as Vicar's Warden. Several of the congregation were employed by the Squire and therefore had little choice but to support him. The Nonconformists were militantly opposed to anything which smacked of 'popery' and so there were many parishioners who were ready to take action to put a stop to these practices, which were totally new to this out-of-the-way Cornish benefice.

Such 'aggrieved parishioners' (as they were officially termed in Church Courts) had a powerful champion for their cause in the Protestant Truth Society, which was founded by Mr. John Kensit in 1890 to resist and stamp out 'Ritualism' and Romanising tendencies in the Church of England. This society had come to the aid of many English parishes in similar difficulties and could always instigate action if they were able to find 'aggrieved parishioners' who were prepared to protest. They inspected the churches concerned, making careful notes of all 'illegal' furnishings and adornments, they attended and protested at services, they held meetings and gathered dossiers of evidence of 'illegalities' to be passed on to the diocesan Bishop for him to take action, Cury-with-Gunwalloe provided a superb case for their crusading zeal and, once informed about Wason, they acted immediately, publicising their activities and findings in the Society's journal, 'The Churchman's Magazine'.

Evidently the PTS had been well-briefed with newspaper reports, including a statement to the 'Western Morning News' in September 1905 by the late Vicar's son, stating 'I have seen the Rev. L. S. Wason who desires me to state that what he does in the celebration of the Eucharist is to interpolate the Canon of the Mass from the Roman Missal. This he sometimes does in English, though preferably in the original (Latin)'. Mr. Churchwarden Martin had also written to the same newspaper in August 1905, stating that the organ was 'practically closed', the choir 'dispersed' and Sunday School 'as extinct as the dodo' and the congregation driven away, adding that 'In no case will any of us Cury parishioners tolerate such services as are now provided for us'. A petition, signed by the Squire and 108 parishioners was prepared and services ranging from Benediction and the Mass of the Presanctified to the Blessing of the Paschal Candle and a Requiem Mass for the late Bishop of Truro were reported.

Mr. John Alfred Kensit travelled down in person to see the churches and was horrified to find that 'the Lord's Table had been made to appear like a Roman Altar', also a locked tabernacle, sanctuary lamp, Latin altar cards, sacring bell, lavabo bowl, Stations of the Cross and Holy Water, also vestments laid out in the vestry, a thurible, Asperges equipment, Roman Catholic hymnbooks and 'But yet more, the Vicar dared to use A ROMAN MISSAL'!

Mr. Kensit's visit was followed by a series of meetings and addresses by his Wickliffe Preachers. After one of these the preacher and his hearers went to the church, where the service of Benediction was taking place behind locked doors (probably locked for fear of interruption). They waited and caught the Vicar and congregation slipping out by the priest's door and challenged them. In the argument which followed the Wickliffe Preacher was nearly pushed into a ditch and when he asked the Vicar what right he had to hold such a service with the doors locked, Wason simply replied in his usual unconcerned way. 'No right at all; no right at all'. All this was considered significant enough for Mr. Kensit to publicise the 'goings on' at Cury in his address to the Church Congress at Barrow-in-Furness that year.

On March 30th 1910, Mr. Kensit wrote to the Bishop of Truro, giving a blow by blow account of the Veneration of the Cross and the Mass of the Presanctified which had taken place at Cury on Good Friday of that year. Clearly Cury's

Cornish country folk had been treated to the full Good Friday liturgy according to the Roman Missal, which included what Protestant stalwarts termed 'Creeping to the Cross' when, as the Churchman's Magazine described, 'the acolyte placed a purple cushion on the steps leading to the "altar" and then the Vicar proceeded to take the draped crucifix from off the "altar" and going to the side uncovered one arm, saying 'Behold the wood of the cross'. The acolyte responded, "O come, let us adore". The other arm was then uncovered and the same words repeated. The whole of the drapery was then removed and the blasphemy repeated by priest and acolyte. The crucifix was then placed on the cushion and the Vicar proceeded to take off his shoes. The organ now struck up, leading the "Crux Fidelis". During the singing the Vicar came down to the chancel and turning towards the crucifix genuflected, then advancing a few paces genuflected again, and the third time, having reached it, bowed down and kissed it. He was followed in this act of idolatry by the elder acolyte . . .' Mr. Kensit expressed some concern that, although some sort of inquiry had been held by the Bishop following the complaints of 1906, no action had been forthcoming.

Bishop Stubbs (who had of course only arrived in the diocese in 1906) immediately replied that he was instructing the Archdeacon of Cornwall to hold a full inquiry into the facts. The result of the inquiry was a letter from the Bishop to Wason (dated 27th April 1910), reminding him of his Oath of Canonical Obedience and his declaration to use only the Book of Common Prayer and none other, except by legal authority, and charging him with breaking his Oath by:-

1. Holding the Mass of the Presanctified. 2. Using incense. 3. Veneration of the image of the Blessed Virgin Mary. 4. Using and teaching prayers and devotions to the Virgin Mary and the saints. 5. Holding an unauthorised service on the Feast of the Assumpton. 6. Similarly on All Souls Day.

He demanded from Wason an assurance that none of these things should happen again, that the Prayer Book only be used for services, except with his special sanction, asked for and granted, and that if he did not receive within three weeks a satisfactory reply, he would inhibit Wason from ministering anywhere in the diocese outside his own parishes. Wason of course ignored the letter and received a further communication from the Bishop, dated June 27th 1910, placing him 'under discipline', which meant that:-

1. The Bishop refused to visit his churches. 2. Wason was banned from all synods and conferences in his Rural Deanery, Archdeaconry and Diocese. 3. He was confined to his parishes and was forbidden to preach or minister in any other parish in the diocese. So that his fellow clergy were aware of this, both letters were published in the press on July 4th.

The 'Churchman's Magazine' rejoiced that the Bishop had exercised such discipline and Mr. Kensit expressed his appreciation, reminding his Lordship of similar illegalities needing action at St. Mary's Penzance and Polruan.

It goes without saying that the Perpetual Curate of Cury-with-Gunwalloe did not have the slightest intention of taking any notice of the Bishop's admonition – and simply carried on as before, causing Mr. Kensit to write again to the Bishop in November, informing him of this, and of the All Souls Day ceremonies at Gunwalloe, describing the catafalque and pall in the church for the Requiem Mass, the procession with incense to the water's edge and 'the mockery of Praying for the Dead and Censing the Sea' which followed. He urged the Bishop to exercise his right to institute legal proceedings against Wason (which Stubbs had deliberately avoided doing after his earlier inquiry). The Bishop replied that he had no intention of prosecuting Wason, which the 'Churchman's Magazine described as 'Another case of episcopal failure'.

1912 saw the enthronement of the Right Rev'd Winfield Oldfield Burrows as Bishop of Truro. He apparently withdrew his predecessor's restrictions upon Wason as an amnesty to the 'lawless cleric'. In order to see whether the amnesty had worked and to 'take suitable action if not', three of Mr. Kensit's Wickliffe Preachers journeyed to Cury to attend the 11.15 a.m. service on Good Friday. Here they witnessed the full Roman ceremonies, including the Veneration of the Cross, where the 'pardoned' Vicar took off his shoes and in his stockinged feet 'thrice made obeisance to the idol'. This time one of the preachers went forward and addressed an official Protest to the Vicar, reminding him in God's name of the vows taken at his institution to the benefice and demanding the immediate discontinuation of 'this illegal service'. Wason stood up and asked the Preachers to leave, but they refused, unless he promised to stop the service. Wason sent for the constable, who arrived after 40 minutes of waiting in silence and said that he had no power to take any action unless some charge was preferred, leaving no choice but to abandon the service. The Preachers sent a telegram to the Bishop, informing him of the action taken.

Returning to Ralph Nelson's account of life in the vicarage and parishes, an important development happened around 1908, when Miss Emma Taylor, who played the organ for Fr. Walke at Polruan, began travelling across to play at Cury and eventually came to live at the vicarage as Housekeeper. She was a talented person, who not only provided the organ accompaniment at services, but also organised a variety of plays and concerts. With her contribution to church life and Compton Mackenzie's thriving Sunday School at Gunwalloe Mission Room, life in the parishes was not all misery and persecution.

In 1911, Ralph left Cury and emigrated to Canada. He states that Fr. Wason was just unable to keep him on at the vicarage, having given so much of the money he had towards the upkeep and furnishing of the churches. Ralph returned however in 1914, at the outbreak of World War I, and married the housekeeper, Emma Taylor at Gunwalloe Church; Ralph was 25 years of age and his bride was 39. He then joined up for military service, but was invalided out of the War and returned to the vicarage. Shortly afterwards their daughter, Stella, was born.

The War took precedence in people's minds and was considered of far greater importance than the antics of their parish priest, so Fr. Wason was left in peace for a time. He was a fluent speaker of French and so was placed on the list of Wartime Interpreters. He also took in French and Belgian refugee children at the vicarage.

It was during the Great War that a few of the more 'extreme' Anglo Catholic churches dared to introduce the short service of Benediction of the Blessed Sacrament. Here the consecrated Host is taken from the tabernacle in which it is reserved and placed in a monstrance, which is set on the altar amidst lighted candles. The service includes two short hymns interspersed by intercessions or a Litany, a Collect and short responses, also Psalm 117. Then the Sacrament, thus exposed in the monstrance, is lifted by the priest, who makes the Sign of the Cross with it over the congregation, thus blessing the people with the Sacrament, before returning the Host to the tabernacle. It must be said that no such service may be found in the Book of Common Prayer, which gives no authority for any such worship of the Sacrament. Also Article 28 of the 39 Articles does not exactly encourage the practice when it states that 'The Sacrament of the Lord's Supper was not by Christ's ordinance reserved, carried about, lifted up, or worshipped'.

Only the most extreme 'Papalist' churches dared to use Benediction at this time, encouraged by the fact that soldiers returning from France had seen it take place in Roman Catholic churches on the Continent and also it was an act of devotion during which people could commit their friends and relations who were fighting in the trenches into God's care. As we shall see, even the English Church Union − vanguard of the Anglo Catholic Movement as it was − nevertheless backed the Bishops in forbidding its use and refused to defend clergy who were disciplined over it. Wason, of course, had used Benediction (or its modified form of 'Devotions') regularly at Cury since his arrival in 1905!

Having received complaints from certain parishioners, Bishop Burrows paid a personal Visitation to Cury on September 19th 1917 to see for himself what was going on and to officially question the Vicar and Churchwardens. When it came to the time for the questions, Wason refused to answer any of them and so the Vicar's Warden, Mr. Thomas, was compelled to do so. He handed the Bishop a short statement expressing the resentment of regular worshippers towards any attempt to stop them worshipping Jesus in the Blessed Sacrament and reminding him of their willingness to follow their Cornish forefathers who resisted the Reformation changes of King Edward VI with their blood. He then answered various questions, informing the Bishop that Benediction was held every Sunday evening, with a congregation of about 30. The 'O Salutaris' and 'Tantum Ergo', also the Versicles, Responses and Collects were sung in Latin and occasionally the Litany of Loretto and the Litany of the Sacred Heart were used.

The Churchwardens of Gunwalloe were then asked to come forward. These were Ralph Nelson and Mr. Williams. The Bishop was told that Dominical Vespers was said in the church on Sundays. Mr. Williams said that Evensong was never held, whereupon Wason protested that Williams never attended any services, so did not know what took place. He added that Matins and Evensong had been said the previous Sunday – both at 3 p.m.! Ralph pointed out that Evensong was sung during the Winter months at the Mission Hall in the Village. It appeared that the Holy Communion had not been celebrated in Gunwalloe Church for about nine months, but it was noted that, as most of the parishioners were Methodists, it was probably impossible for two or three communicants to be gathered together at the same time.

The Bishop both verbally and by letter asked Wason to abandon Benediction, which of course he ignored. He then sent the new Archdeacon of Cornwall – the redoubtable Stamford Raffles Raffles-Flint (Rector of Ladock since 1905) to attend Evening Service at Cury on February 10th 1918 in order to prepare a report to be submitted to a Commission which was being set up to look into Wason's case and to advise the Bishop as to what action to take.

The Archdeacon attended Dominical Vespers, Sermon and Benediction, which included a Litany to the Blessed Virgin Mary and Latin hymns and Responses. The text of the sermon was 'I, if I be lifted up, will draw all men unto me' and Wason explained to the visitors that what they were witnessing was just that – no more and no less. He hoped that they would go back and tell the Bishop that Fr. Wason was preaching what the Prayer Book and the Gospels taught.

The first meeting of the Bishop's Commission took place in St. Mary's Hall, Truro on March 7th 1919, the Members being the Archdeacon of Bodmin (the Ven. H. H. du Boulay), Canon Hassard of Truro Cathedral, Canon H. R. Jennings of

St. John's Penzance, the Rev'd H. R. Coulthard of Breage and Mr. H. Rogers of Helston. About 20 people attended this public meeting and Wason, as we might expect, was conspicuous by his absence. Mr. Percy Barton, a member of the English Church Union, delivered a formal protest that a spiritual matter was being discussed and tried in a secular court.

The Bishop's visit to Cury was reported, also the Archdeacon's visit on February 10th was described in detail, backed up by the People's Warden, Mr. F. R. Freethy, who had also attended the service. A copy of the Roman Catholic 'Westminster Hymnal' was produced in evidence as being the book in use at the church. The proceedings lasted about half an hour, at the end of which the Archdeacon of Bodmin, on behalf of the Commission, stated that there was sufficient evidence showing prima facie grounds for initiating legal proceedings under the Clergy Discipline Act of 1840 against Mr. Wason and that this recommendation should be laid before the Bishop.

Since the Bishop's visit to him in 1917, Wason, far from repenting or stepping into line, had entered into correspondence with his Diocesan, attempting to justify Benediction. He had stated in one letter that this form of worship of Our Lord had the approval of the entire Latin Church, the assent of the Eastern Church and no Archbishop's Authority had been produced against the practice, which also had the support of some African and American Bishops in full communion with the Ecclesia Anglicana. He added that he would, however, give up the particular form complained of, if shown to be unorthodox, providing His Lordship would authorise some more suitable form!

Meanwhile much correspondence was taking place about the subject in the local newspapers, also a series of articles about Benediction and its development by Fr. Wason himself. He even listed twelve arguments for the case against it (from the original institution of the Eucharist to the 39 Articles) and then answered these, one by one. Some of this material took the form of a pamphlet which he had prepared in typescript in 1917, entitled 'Benediction in the Church of England', to be published by Cope & Fenwick. Sadly only part of the typescript has survived.

Back at Cury on Good Friday 1919 there was more trouble. Ralph Nelson records that during the service a group of locals started an argument in the church porch with some of the congregation. Wason went to investigate and a farmer called Richards hit him in the face. Although the wound later required five stitches, Wason returned immediately to the Altar and finished the service with blood streaming down his vestments. He refused his right to prosecute for assault, saying that it is much better that we pray for our enemies.

The 'Trial' itself took place in the crypt of Truro Cathedral on April 25th 1919. The Lord Bishop presided over the proceedings, accompanied by Mr. F. Newbolt, K.C., the Archdeacon of Bodmin and Canon Hassard, with Mr. Hardy appearing for the prosecution. Wason was cited to appear but had no intention of doing so and was not defended. Instead he wrote a letter to the Court, which was handed in by Ralph Nelson, saying 'I intend to absent myself and take no notice of such citation. This is a court no Catholic churchman can recognise. It is neither technically, as your Lordship has admitted in a letter, nor in fact, the Bishop's Consistory Court. It is a grave sin to appear before it. It is a State Tribunal ... But even at this late hour I am still prepared to abide by the decision of the Church Court provided, and I think this only fair under the circumstances, that you will publically disassociate yourself from the present Erastian Substitution'!

A body of Catholic lay-folk were present from St. George's Truro, having attended to make a protest, but the Chancellor would not have the protest read out and instead demanded a written copy, which caused difficulties.

Mr. Hardy in his evidence described the history of the troubles at Cury and Gunwalloe since 1916 and Archdeacon Raffles-Flint again described the service that he had attended there. The Churchwarden, Mr. Freethy, then corroborated this evidence. He said that he was elected by the parishioners to this office (presumably in place of Mr. Bowden the butcher) at the Vestry Meeting in 1911, with 40–50 people present. He added that another Vestry Meeting had taken place in 1912, but that was the last one that he knew of in the parish. The population in 1911 was 359 people in Cury and

152 in Gunwalloe. Despite being People's Warden, he did not attend any services at the church because he took exception to them. (Ralph Nelson said that he had attended two services in twelve years).

Next the document of Wason's Oath of Obedience, signed by him on his arrival in 1905, was produced, followed by Wason's letter explaining his absence. It was Fr. Wason's wish that this should be read out to the Court, but this did not happen.

On May 27th 1919 the Court re-assembled in the Cathedral Chapter Room and the Sentence depriving the Reverend Leighton Sandys Wason from his living was drawn up and signed by the Bishop. Ralph Nelson, after the Sentence had been read out, remarked 'Shameful'! This is by no means the end of the story. Wason firmly believed that whatever a piece of paper from a secular court said to the contrary, he was the rightful incumbent of Cury and Gunwalloe. He had no intention of moving; he would stay put, and carry on as before!

The following week the Bishop of Truro arrived to stay the Saturday night at the Poldhu Hotel, intending to celebrate the Holy Communion in Cury Church on the Sunday. He sent typewritten notices to each of the Churchwardens, Mr. Alfred Thomas, whom Wason had appointed shortly after he had arrived in 1905 and Mr. J. F. Freethy, whom his opponents had elected in 1911. The notices announced that 'The Bishop of Truro proposes to hold the following services in this church on Sunday June 1st 8.0. Holy Communion, 11.0. Mattins and Sermon, 6.30. Evensong'. Mr. Freethy obediently posted his copy on the church door on Friday, but by noon on Saturday it had disappeared. Mr. Thomas's copy was not posted immediately, but was taken to the vicarage, where Wason made a few adjustments using his typewriter and had it placed a little later on the notice board outside the church door. The adjusted version read, 'The Vicar of Cury-with-Gunwalloe (the words 'Bishop of Truro' were crossed out) proposes to hold the following services in this church on Sunday June 1st. 11 ('8' crossed out) Holy Communion AND BENEDICTION (11.0 Mattins crossed out), (6.30 crossed out) Evensong and Sermon at Gunwalloe at 3p.m.'. Ralph Nelson preserved this

piece of paper about what he called 'The Glorious June 1st'
and pasted it in his album, where it may still be seen.

The Bishop had instructed Mr. Freethy to obtain the church
keys to hand over to him on his arrival, but learning that
Freethy was unwell, he declined to trouble him with this task,
trusting that the keys would be surrendered to him by 7.45
a.m. on the Sunday. Upon his arrival to celebrate the Holy
Communion at 8 a.m., he saw Mr. Thomas and asked for the
keys, only to be told that they were at the vicarage. To the
vicarage he duly went, arriving just before 8 a.m. and was
greeted there by Fr. Wason in his pyjamas, calling down to
him through an open upstairs window. Wason told him that
he was not answering any more questions and that he had,
reluctantly, to refuse to hand the keys over, because the
Bishop had taken proceedings against him in an uncanonical
court. He did however suggest a meeting a little later at the
next-door bungalow of a Mr. Fawcus (who formed the third
of a triumvirate with Messrs Sich and Turley Smith,
responsible for the Golf Course and who did not dislike
Wason, but disapproved of his behaviour).

A great many people had turned up to hear the Bishop at
11.0 a.m. and those of them who were hoping for entertain-
ment were not to be disappointed! At 10.45 Fr. Wason
appeared at his parish church dressed in his Eucharistic
vestments and biretta to celebrate Mass as usual. Once inside
the church he was accosted by Mr. Freethy and the Squire,
Major Lee, asking if he intended obstructing the Bishop.
Wason replied that he was not going to discuss this in church
and proceeded to the vestry, whereupon Freethy and Lee went
hot-foot to the bungalow of Mr. Fawcus to report all this to
the Bishop. The churchyard was full of people who refused to
attend Fr. Wason's Mass but were either keen to see what
would happen next, or were genuinely keen to hear their
Bishop. His Lordship decided that he would go to the church
at 11.30 and he told Mr. Freethy to ask the Vicar whether the
church would be available then, but when Freethy arrived, the
service had begun and he thought it best not to interrupt. And
what a service this was going to be! It may have been that Fr.
Wason and his congregation were overflowing with
devotional zeal that Sunday – or possibly that he took

advantage of having the largest congregation in Cury Church for many years, but more likely the astute and irrascible parish priest was determined that the Bishop was NOT going to get the slightest chance of conducting Matins that morning, because Morning Worship at Cury on June 1st 1919 took a very long time indeed! First the Mass was celebrated, then the Altar was prepared for Benediction, which duly took place, then Fr. Wason took his seat in the chancel, before the High Altar, to begin his sermon about the Mysteries of the Ascension. This sermon however was preached in instalments, punctuated by decades of the Rosary, sung in Latin, between each part of it. Freethy, Fawcus and the Bishop made their entrance just after the sermon had begun, followed by most of the 'congregation' from the churchyard − so by now the church was almost full. Wason continued his Homily, occasionally breaking off to remonstrate about people entering or leaving the church during the service. The Bishop waited patiently in the vestry for half an hour and finally at 2.05 p.m. he left the church, together with most of the congregation, leaving a dozen or so 'regulars' to hear the sermon finish. Wason then came down the church and asked a group of people (including Freethy and a constable) if they would kindly close the door when they left. Freethy however demanded the church key and tackled the Vicar about the removal of the Bishop's notice from the door, offering £5 (in the hearing of the spectators in the churchyard) to anybody with information leading to the conviction of the person who took it down.

Wason blissfully ignored all this and in his inimitable, matter-of-fact manner, asked the constable 'Don't you think you might ask these people to go away? I want to go home and have my breakfast'. Freethy again asked for the key, saying that Wason was not intending to hold an evening service and the Bishop therefore wished to. The Vicar replied that he would hand it over if the constable produced a warrant, whereupon the policeman said that he was only there to keep the peace. At this the calm and quick-witted Wason made his departure, saying 'I have been fasting since 6 o'clock (the previous evening) and I will take a cup of tea. Any of you who would like to see me may do so in the vicarage garden'.

He did not have very long for his cup of tea, because he was due at Gunwalloe at 3 p.m., where he had a large congregation, although most of these dwindled away as Benediction began.

The following week the Rev'd Herbert Craven Martin took up residence at Housel Bay, The Lizard, having been appointed by the Bishop to take charge of Wason's parishes. He had just returned to England after 12 years in India as an Army Chaplain and was a sound 'Establishment Low Churchman'. (He was later to succeed the Archdeacon as Rector of Ladock, before becoming Rector of Ockley, Surrey, for 20 years). He did not have much to do on his first two Sundays because Wason forestalled him and said Mass himself, and Martin, rather than cause trouble, quietly went away. Evidently the two priests did meet and Wason observed that Martin was a total stranger to Cornwall, commenting that 'The people will consider it odd that a local Truro clergyman should not have been sent to take charge'.

After two Sundays of the Vicar conducting the services and Mr. Martin quietly withdrawing came the Eve of Corpus Christi (Wednesday June 18th), when Fr. Wason had Benediction at 7 p.m. and then returned to the vicarage, leaving the church unlocked. About 9 p.m. that evening, on the instructions of the Bishop's Legal Advisers, Mr. Freethy, Major Lee and several other interested parishioners, together with a carpenter, fitted a sturdy new lock to the south door of Cury Church and made the north door (which was always bolted) additionally secure by the insertion of a strong screw in the door-jamb. The church was then locked with the new key. Whilst these people were still talking in the churchyard (about 9.30) news of the new lock reached the vicarage and along came Wason, with Mr. Churchwarden Thomas and Ralph Nelson. An 'animated discussion' ensued between the two parties, during which Mr. Freethy refused to let the Vicar have a key to the new lock and informed him that Mr. Martin would be celebrating the Holy Communion at 8 a.m. the following morning. Everybody eventually went home and two policemen stayed on watch at the church until midnight.

Thursday morning came and the church bell rang out at 7.30 a.m., but when the Reverend Mr. Martin, attired in flannel suit, arrived at 7.45, he found the door locked against him. From outside there was no sign of any damage to the door, but inside the lock itself had been smashed to smithereens and the piece of wood which had been put on to support it had been broken away. Commenting to a newspaper reporter, Fr. Wason suggested that 'Doubtless some Saint, sympathising with the "Open Church Movement" had made other arrangements'! What had in fact happened was that a chisel had been skilfully inserted and driven through the key-hole or, as Wason added with a smile, 'Love laugh't at locksmiths'! Mr. Martin, who noticed that Fr. Wason was preparing to conduct the service, stayed for part of it and then went away. It is interesting that no attempt was ever made to 'take over' Gunwalloe Church. Mr. Martin never appeared there and Fr. Wason continued to conduct his Sunday afternoon services there.

It was clear that this ridiculous situation could not be allowed to continue for very much longer and Mr. Kensit of the Protestant Truth Society (who had previously sent a telegram to the Bishop, congratulating him upon his treatment of Wason) sent two of his Wickliffe Preachers – Mr. W. H. Benbow and Mr. A. Carley – to help the aggrieved parishioners to sort things out and to keep watch over the church. On Friday June 20th a notice was posted by the Bishop's supporters of a Vestry Meeting the following evening to elect Churchwardens. Mr. Freethy arrived at the church that afternoon and found two Sisters of Mercy there. He had arranged for yet another lock to be fitted and, during its installation, who should appear but the Vicar, together with the Rev'd Reginald Wynter, who was staying with him, together with some of the regular congregation, bringing *their* new lock – but they were just too late, and had to watch 'the Bishop's lock' being screwed in. Fr. Wynter was doubtless extremely interested in the happenings at Cury, because he was about to be 'visited' by the Bishop of Bath & Wells over the subject of Benediction at his church of St. John's Taunton and was himself forced to leave his parish the following year.

The Vestry Meeting began at 8.30 p.m. in the Schoolroom and the Rev'd H. C. Martin presided over a large audience, which included the Rev'd Fathers Sandys Wason and

Reginald Wynter! Mr. Martin said that he had been placed
in charge by the Bishop and asked for a vote of support,
which he received. Wason's hand was raised in support; to
him it was totally stupid and also illegal, because the meeting
did not have the statutory three days' notice. Major Lee was
reinstated (after 14 years) as Vicar's Warden, with Mr.
Freethy as People's Warden. Then followed a procession to
the parish church formally to take it over. Fr. Wason had
been granted permission to go into the building to remove his
Missal. He had already removed the church plate and registers
without permission and refused to return them. He
commented to a newspaper reporter that when he took Fr.
Wynter to show him the church on the Saturday evening, they
were refused entry by six Nonconformist farmers and two
Wickliffe Preachers, also that Mr. Freethy had told Ralph
Nelson and Alfred Thomas that if they were ever seen within
the church precincts, he would not be responsible for the
consequences. A vigil (but not in the liturgical sense!) was
kept at the church throughout Saturday night (several of the
invigilators, according to Ralph Nelson, being much the
worse for liquor) and the Vicar heard the church bells ringing
at 2.30 a.m.

Evidently that night the Protestants had a thorough 'purge'
of the church interior. According to Ralph Nelson, Our
Lady's statue was 'dragged down and stuffed away up the
tower, with many coarse oaths and rude jests'. The crucifix
received the same treatment and the sanctuary lamp was
pulled down and overturned. He adds that 'The Blessed
Sacrament remained on the altar during all that dreadful night
and only by appealing to the man Martin were we allowed to
go and consume it'. Fr. Wason later stated that he asked Mr.
Martin if he might go into the church on the Sunday morning
to remove the Sacrament, and was given three minutes in
which to do so. It seems that a sturdy broom had to be hastily
procured on the Sunday morning to brush up the cigarette and
cigar ends which littered the church, before Morning Prayer
could be said.

Mr. Martin's Matins drew a large congregation, described
by Wason as 'an enthusiastic complication of Nonconformists and Wickliff's Preachers'. The candlesticks had been

removed from the Holy Table, which was covered with a white cloth; the Lady Chapel was bare.

Having removed the church plate and registers to the Vicarage, Fr. Wason set up an Oratory Chapel in one of the rooms, equipped so that 'lawful services' could continue to be conducted by the 'lawful parish priest'. The following notice was posted in the window of a workshop beside the church, informing parishioners that 'The Perpetual Curate of Cury-with-Gunwalloe, having been forcibly and illegally prevented from entering the Parish Church, hereby gives notice that Mass will be said by him as the lawful Pastor at the vicarage on Sunday next, June 22nd, at 8 and 11 a.m. Sandys Wason'. A letter from him dated June 24th, which appeared in the local newspapers, made his position clear – 'Sir: Uncanonically deprived from the benefice of Cury-with-Gunwalloe and now forbidden access to the church by force majeure, it may be asked "Why retain a temporality, the vicarage, when you can no longer exercise the spiritual authority you still claim?" I remain here, until ejected, to celebrate the Holy Mysteries and to dispense the Sacraments to the faithful. A temporary Oratory has been fitted up here, and is the only place where the Sacraments may be lawfully administered'.

The mention of the possibility of ejection in this letter indicates that Wason expected that this might finally happen. He could hardly have imagined the horror of the events which actually did take place when the time came.

Meanwhile, the news of Fr. Wason's deprivation spread quickly and drew the interest of church-folk outside Cornwall. Extreme Protestants hailed it as a triumphant victory for the Reformed Church against the machinations of Popery. Many Prayer Book Catholics and even those more 'extreme' were sorry, but not surprised, because Benediction was totally Roman and Continental, and most of those who would have liked to use the service would never have dared to do so. Even the English Church Union (of which Fr. Wason was not a member) issued a statement that it was unable to take any action on his behalf, that his behaviour in the matter was not such as the Union could approve of, that because its aim was to seek to 'defend and maintain unimpaired the

doctrine and discipline of the Church of England' it could not
oppose a Bishop exercising his canonical authority, and it
could not defend Benediction as an appointed service of the
English Church.

Many Anglican Catholics however did not share this view
and a demonstration took place shortly after the sentence was
passed in Caxton Hall, Westminster, when the hall was
'packed to asphyxiation-point' long before the meeting began
and an overflow meeting took place in Christ Church,
Victoria Street. The Duke of Newcastle was to have chaired
the meeting but was not able to attend, so sent a letter which
was read out by Col. Dampier who replaced him. A reporter
noted that 'one saw intensely respectable middle-aged ladies
sitting in cramped attitude on the floor' – so crowded was the
auditorium.

The first priest to address the gathering was the Rev'd
Conrad Noel, the outspoken champion of Christian
Socialism, who gave a glowing account of the Corpus Christi
processions held in and around his glorious church at
Thaxted, where he also had Benediction, saying that people
must fight for it whether they liked it or not. Fr. Alban H.
Baverstock spoke next. He had known Fr. Wason for over 20
years, and his oratory roused the meeting to a 'state of intense
enthusiasm'. He said that it was true that Benediction was not
ordered in the Prayer Book – but neither was the 'elevation
of the almsdish' at the collection! He was followed by Fr.
Ernest Kilburn of St. Saviour's Hoxton, who urged that
Wason should be supplied with the means to stay at Cury,
adding 'I am here because I believe that Fr. Wason is doing
what he ought to do.' When Fr. Arthur Tooth rose to his feet,
it was to tumultuous applause. He had been persecuted,
prosecuted, deprived of his living, locked out of his church
and even imprisoned in Horsemonger Lane Gaol for his
'ritualist practices'.

Finally, Fr. Wason stood up and acknowledged the kind
things which had been said about him by his brother priests.
A guarantee fund was inaugurated to support him so long as
he remained under sentence of deprivation and continued to
administer the Sacraments at Cury and Gunwalloe.

The Vicarage under Siege

He who remained adamant that he was still the lawful
Perpetual Curate of Cury-with-Gunwalloe (which he main-
tained throughout his life), who was described by his ever
faithful friend and Churchwarden, Ralph Nelson as 'a quiet
and inoffensive priest, who made himself poor for the sake of
his small flock' was now without the support of any stipend or
income. He remained however in the home which he believed
was rightfully his and offered the Holy Eucharist with his
small congregation in his vicarage oratory.

The album of photographs and comments which Ralph
compiled contains several scenes from this period, including a
party 'during the siege of the vicarage', a picture of the
Oratory Chapel, a photograph of Wason, cigarette in mouth
and saw in hand, with the caption 'Fr. Wason, deprived of his
living, takes to wood-sawing and trying to make ends meet by
saving coal', a picture of Ralph himself, with trilby hat and
shotgun, outside the vicarage 'on guard the week that the
Bishop's supporters were to come and turn us out', also a
photograph of Sheila, the donkey, with rider, 'who were both
well-stoned and generally made to feel uncomfortable', which
was taken two days before her burial.

Sheila was the little donkey who used to take members of
the vicarage household to Helston to get the shopping and
conveyed them around the parishes. Because she had grown
very old and was being 'pushed around by some of the louts',
Wason felt that the time had come when her life should be
humanely ended. She was buried in a shady spot in the
vicarage garden. The knowledge of her burial provided an

excellent execuse for those who objected to the deposed Vicar remaining in their midst to cause trouble, and so it was that the surprised residents of the vicarage found the Sanitary Inspector on their doorstep, demanding that the carcass should be dug up for inspection. The Inspector was nevertheless quite satisfied with the burial and Sheila was again laid to rest. On the night of July 9th however a group of local antagonists dug up the decaying carcass and dragged it in front of Fr. Wason's window. The smell on that humid Cornish summer's night must have been terrible. The following morning a firm of people who dealt in animal carcasses was summoned to take the remains away.

It was inevitable that some attempt should be made to remove the residents of the vicarage from their home and on Thursday October 2nd the 'end' came. At 10.30 a.m. there was a knock on the door and, just in case it was a sick call, the knock was answered. Instead Major Lee, Mr. Freethy and several burly Cornish farmers entered the vicarage to take possession of it and to eject the Vicar, who was told that they had brought wagons to convey his furniture wherever he desired it to be taken. Wason said that he would go if they could produce a legal warrant and then asked Ralph to cycle to Helston to get the police, but his exit was barred by a dozen or so villagers, who also removed and immobilised his bicycle. Wason had as his guest at the vicarage his cousin, Geoffrey Biddulph, who slipped out unnoticed, commandeered one of the villagers' bicycles and rode to Helston, but the police there refused to take action because it was a Church matter.

The farmers and villagers immediately turned their attention to removing the furniture, beginning in the dining room, where breakfast was being laid and sweeping the contents of the table into a potato-sack. The contents of the Oratory were thrown into a heap on the floor. Emma Nelson and little 4½ year old Stella retreated to their bedroom but before long several men had entered and stripped it, stuffing the mother's and child's clothing into coal-boxes alongside bottles of ink. At one stage of the proceedings Ralph barred one of the doors so that they could have some respite and some food, but a parishioner called Mr. Pengelly used a large log of wood as a battering-ram to force it open.

In the middle of all this turmoil the Rev'd Thomas Godfrey, Vicar of Holy Trinity Hoxton, who was staying at Mullion, arrived as a guest for lunch, blissfully ignorant of what awaited his arrival, having been invited several days before. Snippets from his written and signed account show how frightening the situation was: –

'The poor Father, in all his distress, with his usual unselfishness and good nature, insisted on my having something to eat. So, to satisfy him, I started munching some bread and jam which I foraged for myself from an upturned box in the kitchen.' He continues by stating that twice the uninvited 'guests' ordered him out of the house, but he refused, saying that as Fr. Wason's guest it was up to him alone to ask him to leave. They then laid hands upon him and pushed him out. 'About five minutes after that, Fr. Wason came out to put some of his belongings into the taxi. When he tried to get into the house again, the Nonconformist Churchwarden stood at the door with outstretched arms and refused to let him go in, though he protested that his money, as well as several personal belongings, were within. I believe his bag was thrown out. Anyhow, I next saw him stooping down to put something into the bag, when one of the ruffians struck him on the head and threw off his hat with a malicious laugh. Their conduct was more like that of animals than that of civilised human beings.'

The locals worked non-stop and the furniture was finally loaded about 2 p.m. A motor-taxi was on hand to convey Fr. Wason, Ralph, Emma, Stella, Geoffrey Biddulph and the bull-terrier wherever they wished. The Vicar surrendered the plate and registers upon demand. He later told a reporter that the Rev'd Martin had once given his word that no force would ever be used to remove him. Judging from Mr. Martin's behaviour towards Fr. Wason at other times, one suspects that he had no part in it whatsoever. 'I am,' said Fr. Wason to the reporter, 'on the world – I have no employment'.

That afternoon the taxi, with its sad and battered occupants, set off for Fr. Walke's vicarage at St. Hilary, followed at a much slower speed by three horse-drawn wagons, loaded with furniture etc., which arrived at St. Hilary about 7 p.m.

The story is continued by Fr. Walke, who had been very

concerned for his old friend for some time and had daily feared and expected news of an attack upon Cury vicarage. On the fateful day the taxi drew up and out climbed Fr. Wason, in cassock and biretta, followed by Emma Nelson, brandishing a toilet-roll. Having entered the house, Fr. Wason, his face ashen white, firstly pointed to some candlesticks on Walke's mantelpiece and said 'You must have yellow candles in there, Ber' and then asked if he might convey the Holy Oils he had rescued to St. Hilary Church.

Upon his return, he remarked 'Stupid people. Dreadful, dreadful to have disturbed your party'. After dark the wagons arrived with the furniture – each drawn by two horses and loaded high. Wason, who by this time was deep into a game of chess with one of Fr. Walke's guests, refused to show any interest in their arrival. 'Don't be fussy', he said, 'It is clergymanly to get fussy. Sit down and watch the game. Most interesting.' Meanwhile all his worldly possessions were being piled haphazardly in the courtyard in the pouring rain, together with living and squashed specimens from the huge epidemic of caterpillars which had recently invaded Cury vicarage.

Later that evening, much of the furniture had been carried up three flights of stairs and stored in an empty upper room, and beds were prepared for Wason, the Nelsons and Geoffrey Biddulph, who were to remain at St. Hilary for several months. That is, apart from Fr. Wason himself, who after the early Mass next morning was ready with his suitcase, determined to return forthwith to Cury. 'Must be there to say Mass for those stupid people', he said, 'Can't do anything else for them'. Fr. Walke commented in his account of these events, 'All this happened 15 years ago, but Fr. Wason has not forgotten and still devotes his Sunday Mass to the same "stupid people"'.

He managed to stay at Mullion, where his friend, neighbour and fellow Catholic, Fr. James Scholefield, was Vicar. For a period he lodged there with the Tonkin family and Mr. Stanley Tonkin (who has been a Server at Mullion Church for 58 years and its Churchwarden for 15 years) remembers Father Wason being taken in by his parents for a few months. His brother had served for Wason and had taken part in the

All Souls processions. Fr. Scholefield allowed his fugitive friend to celebrate the occasional weekday Mass at the Lady Altar in Mullion Church and the young Stanley served for him; he remembers having to learn the Kyries in Greek in order to do so.

Stanley Tonkin remembers Fr. Wason with great affection – especially his genuine love of and delight in youngsters. Whilst at Mullion (and then aged 52), nothing pleased him more than the chance to join in the lads' games of football. He even took a pair of his trousers and cut them into shorts so that he could really look the part when he participated in this ad-hoc village soccer!

After his return from St. Hilary, he celebrated Mass for a while in the cottage of his faithful ex-Churchwarden, Mr. Alfred Thomas. This clearly annoyed his opponents in the parish, who attacked the cottage on the night of October 6th, with 'clods, old kettles and stones', effecting considerable damage and breaking several windows.

Ralph Nelson and his family eventually moved to Bodmin, where he became gardener for the Rev'd Raleigh Gilbert and faithfully supported Bodmin's great church of St. Petrock for 45 years. At the end of his album of accounts and pictures of his Cury days, he wrote a note summarising the events and concluding with the remark that Fr. Wason was deprived of his living 'the excuse being that he held up the Blessed Sacrament and taught his people to worship it, and blessed them with the consecrated Host. The facts as shown in this album are true and, sad as it is, much more dreadful things could be written. Thomas Ralph Nelson.'

Towards the middle of October 1919, a pamphlet appeared, entitled 'A Few Facts which Speak for Themselves'. It contained a letter from Fr. Wason to the Administrators and Clergy of the Truro Diocese, dated October 6th and explaining that he was temporarily lodging at Mullion Vicarage (unfortunately not in his parish as he should be, but these were exceptional circumstances), but was celebrating Mass at Mr. Thomas's cottage. He asked if his 'rev confreres of the diocese' would offer the Holy Sacrifice for him and help him by their charitable prayers, also maybe materially – which could be sent to Mr. W. J. Buck, 15 Second Avenue, Acton

Park, London W. The pamphlet also included a letter to the
Western Morning News from Ralph Nelson, describing the
'eviction', a report to a newspaper interview given by Wason
and the signed statement by Fr. Godfrey, parts of which have
been quoted earlier. It ends with an appeal for people to help
'in any way you think best'.

Wason the Wanderer –
Life after Cury

After a while, Fr. Wason returned to live in London where, we are told, he had inherited from Mr. A. E. Manning Foster, F.R.S.L., a small firm of Church Publishers, called Cope & Fenwick, which operated firstly from 8 Buckingham Street, Strand and later from Old Burlington Street. The firm was later purchased from Wason by Mr. Lance Scott (and this provided him with a little capital), who then employed him as Manager for £1 per week.

The firm was established in 1906 and its catalogue for 1919–20 shows that Wason thoroughly approved of most of its publications as much as he did of its name! Several books and pamphlets promoting Benediction were produced, also a series of Liturgies from the Eastern Churches, several devotional books and anthologies compiled by Manning Foster himself and works by Fr. A. H. Baverstock and other Catholic stalwarts. By contrast there were also three books about the Bahai Faith.

Wason told Fr. Walke that the name of the firm was 'most distinguished' and 'bound to bring customers' – and he began to speak proudly of himself as 'Cope & Fenwick', delighted at having joined the inner circles of what booksellers call 'the Trade'. When Fr. Walke became concerned about his well-being, he told him 'You are not in the Trade and it is impossible for you to understand the business'. The rented premises (a back-room of the Medici Society) had a little shop which sold devotional books, also statues, crucifixes, rosaries and other objects of devotion, referred to as 'pieties'. He seems to have had very few customers in the shop however and rarely encouraged anybody to buy anything. According to Walke, prospective customers, finding him lost in his Breviary, would be greeted with 'What do you want? — Nothing here. All rubbish', whereupon he would return to his office.

Laura Knight, an artist friend of the Walkes, was persuaded by him to have an exhibition in the shop, which was transformed for a while into a miniature art gallery. He was assisted in this by a Mrs. Miriam Plichta, with whom he spent most of his time playing chess, when not reading his Offices. A very distinguished and well-known patron of the Arts was unwise enough to come in and view the exhibition whilst they were engaged in a game. Expecting to be immediately recognised, this lady approached the table, waited silently, and then remarked 'Chess is a very absorbing game'. 'Very' replied Wason — then 'Check!' to Madame Plichta — and they carried on with the game.

During Wason's time the firm moved to Duke Street, Piccadilly, where the late Horace Keast, the author and authority on Anglo Catholic Cornwall, visited it to look at some rosaries — only to be told 'Why come here? Go somewhere else. They have better selections. I want to get back to my Office'. But Keast persevered, telling Wason that he had been present at the noon Mass celebrated by him the previous day at St. Mary's, Graham Street (now Bourne Street). Fr. Humphrey Whitby, its Vicar, was very generous to Wason, paying him from his own money, but allowing him to believe that it came out of a fund. Fr. Wason would earn the occasional small fee for saying Mass at St. Mary's. Horace Keast had attended the Sunday noon 'Mass with Music', where the priest celebrated inaudibly with the organist playing suitable music throughout. 'Did you hear me?' asked Wason. 'No Father,' replied Keast, 'the music was just a bit too loud'. 'A pity' was the reply, 'It was a proper Mass — in Latin of course'. He then thawed somewhat and talked to Keast about 'those stupid people at Cury whom I always remember in my Sunday Mass for the people'.

Cope & Fenwick was of course very useful to Wason as a

means of publishing some of his writings, especially his novel 'Palafox' in 1927 ... He had long left the book trade when the typed notice was issued in 1946 announcing that Geoffrey Handley Taylor and Ralph Appleyard had resigned as Director and Secretary of Cope & Fenwick and directing all future communications to Edward Halliburton of Edinburgh.

During the 1930s and 40s we find Fr. Wason popping up all over the country! He was very much 'on the road' for the rest of his life and rarely settled anywhere for very long. He spent periods staying with friends and sympathetic parish priests who could use his help and maybe pay him a small fee for taking services. Occasionally he rented a home for a short period — and then moved on again. It was not until 1943 that any Diocesan Bishop would license him to officiate in an English church, but he had many friends amongst the Anglo Catholic clergy and was never without the use of an altar. A host of addresses are given for him during the 30s and 40s, including Rectories and Vicarages at Mumby, near Alford, East Wittering, near Chichester, Cromwell, Notts, etc. Several of the clergy who entertained him were of the old-fashioned Catholic vintage, who remained in one parish for most of their active ministry, like Fr. Mitchell at Mumby (1918–63), Fr. Dallas at Tilbrook, Hunts (1923–?), Fr. Hargrave Thomas at Needham Market (1925–63), Fr. Dolman at Cromwell (1918–56) and Fr. Patrick Shaw at All Saints York (1904–50).

During the 1920s and early 30s he frequently travelled to stay with Fr. Robert Stapylton and his family at Clifford, near Boston Spa, in Yorkshire, where he took duty at the unusual early Gothic Revival church (built in 1842) on the edge of the village. He was doubtless also fascinated by the imposing neo-Romanesque Roman Catholic Church of St. Edward down in the village street. Fr. Stapylton was Vicar from 1917–32 and he revived and developed the Catholic tradition, doing much to beautify the church. Previously he had been Rector of Lolworth, Cambs and then of Whitstone, Cornwall. Whilst at Whitstone, Fr. Wason had invited him to preach at Cury and had reprimanded him for continually saying 'er' whilst preaching — adding 'I shall drop a book every time you say it' — and it appears that he did!

Lady Bingley, the daughter of Lord Halifax, was a stalwart of Clifford Church (she presented it with a crucifix in memory of her father in 1934) and it seems that poor Wason was not too good at getting up to celebrate the early weekday Masses. The housekeepr soon had him out of bed however, by banging on his door and shouting 'Lady Bingley's in church, waiting for Mass' whether she was or not!

He occasionally returned to St. Hilary to see the Walkes and to take part in Fr. Walke's famous plays which, from 1927, were broadcast by the BBC, Wason played Caiaphas in the Passion Play, although during the rehearsals and performances he would remain looking totally disinterested until he was needed – and then he was a considerable liability to the Producer because he would not speak loudly enough, or would not get near enough to the microphone – much to the amusement of the St. Hilary Players, who knew him well. As soon as he had said his piece, out came the Breviary and he was back reciting the Office, dead to the world, and at the earliest possible opportunity he would slip out silently. Fr. Jolly, the Rector of St. Enoder, who played Judas in the Passion Play and Simon Bray in the Eve of All Souls Play, said that at rehearsals he was 'cantankerous to a degree which worried Bernard Walke almost to illness'.

In 1922, Grace Emily Costin (later to become Mother Teresa, the Foundress of the Franciscan Servants of Jesus and Mary at Posbury St. Francis, Devon) arrived at St. Hilary, where she ran a Home for orphan children, known as the 'Jolly Tinners'. She saw a fair amount of Wason on his visits to the Walkes and despaired of him running a bookshop in London with absolutely no business sense. She had first encountered him in Kent, when Fr. Walke suggested that he might visit the Reformatory School which she was running to say Mass once a month. She remembers how chary he was of the girls and how he did his best to keep away from them. On one of his visits, four of them had absconded, having first cut the telephone wires and upset the electric light. Late in the evening she found Wason sitting in the dark, having a quiet smoke. Upon hearing that the girls had not been caught and that the trouble would not be over until midnight, he said 'Well, if you will give me a candle, I will go to bed. You have my prayers'!

Once she wrote to him at the bookshop requesting some Christmas Cards and sending 10 shillings in payment for them. A month later they arrived, with a bill for 10 shillings. She rightly protested by letter about paying twice and received the reply, 'Yes, I remember, most kind of you. I must have torn up the ten shilling note with the letter'. On a visit to the shop he told her that he had St. Teresa of Avila's Autobiography, which would interest her. When she thanked him, but confessed that she could not afford it, he said, somewhat irritably 'My dear Grace, I'm not asking you to buy it. I will give it to you'.

He liked to go to her house for dinner whilst staying at St. Hilary, and this rather irritated Fr. Walke, who asked him why — to which his friend replied honestly and without any intention of rudeness, 'Well, if you must know, it is because Grace puts on a much better dinner than you do'.

It was in the churchyard at St. Hilary on a summer afternoon in 1932 that Frank Baker first encountered him, dressed in cassock and biretta, his monocle swinging from its black cord, trowel in hand and bending over some tiny plant which had caught his interest, the stub of the inevitable cigarette dying away in its holder. Encountering the stranger, Wason ordered, 'Get me some cigarettes, will you!' — which entailed a considerable walk into the village for Frank, who returned later, only to find that Wason had previously despatched somebody else, who had returned first. However Frank's 20 Players were also gratefully accepted, although there was never any offer of payment for them! This marked the start of a deep friendship between the two writers, involving many meetings at St. Hilary and, in 1939—40, actually sharing a house together in Newport, Monmouthshire.

This was in fact a Council House in Rockfield Street, which Wason had acquired about 1937 and had named 'La Chaise Jaune' after a Van Gogh painting. On his first Holy Saturday there, he had the house solemnly blessed by Canon John Cottrell, Vicar of St. Julian's Church, Newport, although he wrote in a letter 'I am already tired of being a householder! No doubt I shall like it in time.'

During his time at 'La Chaise', he was assisting Fr. Cottrell at St. Julian's. This much-loved priest had arrived as its curate when St. Julian's was part of its mother parish and, between 1901–1915 had built up its congregation to become a Conventional District, of which he was Curate in Charge, from 1915–1921, when it became a parish in its own right and he was its first Vicar, from 1921–1940. The Parish History mentions Fr. Wason 'setting off for church in cassock and biretta, white plimsolls on his feet, a monocle in his eye, a popular newspaper and a Latin Breviary under his arm'. He must surely have loved this beautiful church, consecrated in 1926 – its interior dominated by the High Altar and mighty reredos with which Father Ignatius had adorned his Monastery Church at Capel-y-Ffyn, and which was brought here stone by stone in 1932.

Frank Baker, in his book 'The Road was Free', recalls life with Wason at 'La Chaise' – how he would call him in the mornings to say Mass, and be greeted by the vision of a mountain of disordered blankets on the bed and 'projecting from the midst of them, like a periscope from a stormy sea, the tip of his cigarette holder, crumbling away in a tower of ash'! Also the shopping trips into down-town Newport, when he ordered Frank to stop an errand-boy on a bicycle, clutching a long slender apple barrel, in order to find out where he got the barrels so that he could acquire one for use as a linen basket. He also gives us pictures of Wason peeling a large dessert pear with a shoe-horn and of him keeping supper-guests waiting outside in the snow whilst he 'neatly converted pages of The Times into peak-hat table-napkins'.

There is also the story of the search for 'Eggs' – the lost manuscript of Wason's novel 'Storm in an Egg Cup', about a scientist who had found a way of making synthetic eggs. This was written at 'La Chaise' and one of the finished copies was sent to America, never to be returned, whilst the other was mistakenly thrown out by Wason in 1940, with waste-paper bound for the Newport war-time paper salvage depot. He posted a notice on the front door, offering five shillings to any Boy Scout who could manage to recover the precious manuscript from the masses of paper in the depot – and several tried, but without success. After a week, Wason could stand it no longer and insisted upon going himself, so he and Frank proceeded to the huge barn near the A.R.P. Station.

Despite the Warden's warning to Frank 'Don't you let that old man in there with that fag-end in his mouth', Wason unlocked the door and was in — regardless of the avalanche of paper which landslided and almost engulfed him. Having foraged for hours through the whole of Newport's salvage for the past year (piled some 20 feet high) he emerged defeated and gave up — so 'Eggs' was never published.

Fr. Cottrell retired in 1940 and it seems that his successor was not so eager for Wason's help. In 1941, having just had the kitchen redecorated, new curtains ordered and a blue carpet cut specially to fit one of the rooms, Wason decided to move on. He wrote in a letter to a friend 'I have a wireless at La Chaise now. Shall be sorry for some reasons leaving it, but though I've offered to help — no response on his part though he is very friendly'.

During the 1930s Fr. Wason made visits to the delightful and idyllic village of Swainby, set at the foot of the Cleveland Hills in the North Riding of Yorkshire. He lodged at a house called 'the Poplars' and did periods of duty for the Rev'd Algernon Barker at Swainby's Victorian Church of the Holy Cross and at his Mission Church in the nearby hamlet of Potto. Fr. Barker was here from 1917–1950 and, although not as extreme as Wason, he nourished his small community with gentle Catholic teaching, introducing Eucharistic vestments, a Sung Mass every Sunday and also Swainby's beautiful rood screen and rood — believed to be one of the last works of the architect Temple Moore.

From his letters it is clear that Fr. Wason enjoyed his periods of duty in this picturesque place. Of the little Mission Church he says, 'Potto is unspeakably charming'. He enjoyed visiting the sick, administering the weekly Communion, befriending the young folk (whom he referred to throughout his ministry as 'the lambs' and those slightly older as 'the buddies') and doing a spot of writing in these lovely surroundings. His letters speak of sledging on the snow-covered hills with the 'lambs', having to conduct Morning Prayer, giving away crosses with sermonettes and finding it 'a great relief having 2 Lay Readers reading the Lessons'. He added that, 'I have told Mrs. Barker, once or twice, that she coddles the people — she most surely mothers me'!

1942 found Fr. Wason attending the Corpus Christi celebrations at Cromwell, near the A1 in Nottinghamshire, where he occasionally did duty for his friend Fr. William Dolman in the village church. Here the Fynes Clinton family have several memorials and had been Patrons and occasionally Rectors. He stayed at the Rectory (now a fascinating Dolls' Museum) where Fr. H. J. Fynes-Clinton (the Papalist Rector of St. Magnus the Martyr in the City of London and one-time Priest Director of the Catholic League) had lived as a boy.

One ordinand at the Corpus Christi service remembered Wason sitting through the whole of Solemn Vespers, apparently oblivious to all that was going on, reading his Breviary. Afterwards the visitor shook hands with him and received his Blessing in Latin. The following year he met Wason again at High Mass in West Retford Parish Church. Afterwards, when told how the Archdeacon of Lindsey was persecuting Catholic priests in the Skegness area, he suggested that people should obtain rubber stamps with the legend 'Made in Germany' and stamp these words upon every copy of the Book of Common Prayer that they could lay their hands upon!

A great friend of Fr. Wason was Fr. Patrick Shaw, who was Rector of All Saints, North Street, York, from 1904–1950. All Saints is one of the most atmospheric churches in this wonderful city of ancient churches. Set in alleys west of the river, its thin 120 foot spire rises above the buildings in what is left of this 'olde-worlde' corner. We can imagine Wason in his element in this eccentric church, with its leaning walls and arcades, its Stations of the Cross framed and painted upon wood to look like Old Masters, the light-coloured and beautifully carved wooden screen, by E. Ridsdale Tate (1908), surmounted by a Rood and enclosing return stalls, the ancient roofs with their mediaeval angels, and what is probably the most beautiful array of 14th and 15th century glass in any parish church in the land.

Attached to the west end of the church is the Anker Hold – a little upper room of reinforced shuttered concrete clad with timber-framing, with an attractive bay-window to the north. Designed by Ridsdale Tate and built around 1906, it was intended to be a place where people in desperate need of a roof over their heads could stay. This was of course an ideal 'bolt-hole' for Fr. Wason on his travels and, over a period of some 7−8 years, he was often in residence there, doing duty for Fr. Shaw and assisting in his busy round of services and parochial duties. Sunday services at All Saints were advertised as Matins at 8.30 a.m., then Sung Litany in procession, Solemn Mass at 9, followed by Thanksgiving after Communion at 10.45, Sunday School at 3 p.m. and Solemn Evensong at 6.30. There was daily Mass at 7.15 a.m. and Evensong at 6.30 (Solemnly sung on Saturdays at 9 p.m.). The Angelus was advertised at 6.30 a.m., 12 noon and 6.30 p.m., also daily Confessions at noon and on Saturdays at 6.30 p.m. Nearby, All Saints ran a Church House, Church Shop (selling books and aids to devotion) and Laundry. The church also appears to have owned the pair of brick and timber cottages in All Saints Lane, near the east end of the church, because Fr. Wason occasionally occupied No. 1 when the Anker Hold was not vacant.

Fr. Peter Blagdon-Gamlen who, as a young Officer, occasionally served his Masses at All Saints, remembers him darting into the church to fetch the stole from the confessional in order to bless a new Rosary for him and emerging clad in it over his outdoor clothes. Typical of Wason, having shot back in to return the stole, he emerged still wearing it, having absent-mindedly replaced his umbrella in the confessional instead.

Also very much attached to All Saints was Miss Margaret Elizabeth Hay Deas (known as Daisy), whose appearance and eccentricity almost outdid Wason's! They had known each other since the 1930s and most of Fr. Wason's surviving letters were written to her. She took it upon herself to look after (and maybe also to manage) him when he was in York. She was a passionate lover of animals and spent much of her time in the Church Shop and in the church itself. She lived at 48 Micklegate, one of a terrace of Georgian houses, above what is now the Oxfam Shop.

The early 1940s, with World War II well under way, saw Fr. Wason transferring his attentions from Wales to East Anglia. A letter, dated S. Pius V 1941 (i.e. May 5th) and headed 'St.

Bartholomew's Vicarage, Ipswich — where I hope to go on Wednesday or Thursday' tells of the great welcome he received at this grand church, which from its consecration in 1895 has been a Catholic stronghold. He knew its Vicar Fr. Claude Powell who, according to the letter, allowed him to say Mass daily. At that time he was leading a rather busy life, because since the previous Holy Week he writes 'I've been to Felpham (Sussex) helping — for Easter 2 Masses — some 3 or 4 hundred communicants — then to Ipswich — Cambridge — Ipswich — Newport'. Later in 1941 he had settled into 29 Felixstowe Road, Ipswich — the home of St. Bartholomew's Curate, the Rev'd Stanley L. Davis during the Autumn of 1942, before he left to be an RNVR Chaplain. He even had visiting cards printed giving this address. In a letter (probably to Fr. Shaw) from No. 29, he mentioned work with cadets from the nearby H.M.S. Ganges, an Air Raid the previous night with '2 Bombs and 4 Houses gone west but DG no casualties' and the progress of Fr. Powell's son and of other people connected with him.

It was not until 1942 (i.e. 23 years after he was deprived of his living) that any Diocesan Bishop gave him a Licence under Seal to officiate legally in an Anglican church in his diocese. The Bishop who licensed him that year was the Right Rev'd Richard Brook of St. Edmundsbury and Ipswich and the parish priest who used his influence to facilitate this was the Rev'd W. G. Hargrave Thomas, who was Vicar of Needham Market from 1925 – 1963. Fr. Hargrave Thomas was a caring and devoted parish priest and a musician of no mean ability, although he was a controversial character in Suffolk because of his Anglo-Catholicism and his crusading Socialism. He invited Fr. Wason to come to Necdham Market as his Assistant Priest. At that time the cottage beside the old School House (11 King William Street) was vacant, and Wason duly moved in. Here he had a kitchen, front room and three bedrooms, but no washbasin — the water having to be carried in from the pump.

He celebrated Mass at Needham Market for the first time on December 6th 1942 and from then onwards he celebrated on every possible Saint's Day. Usually two communicants only were recorded — probably Hargrave Thomas and himself. The initials 'S.W.' appear in the Services Register for the last time on September 2nd 1943. The Parish Magazine for January 1943 announced his arrival, saying 'we are glad to have the presence of such a learned and experienced priest'. The March issue announced a Lent Course of Sermons on Sunday mornings after the Sung Mass — a spiritual conference, conducted by Father Wason. In August, thanks were recorded to him for all his help during the absence of the parish priest.

His letters to Daisy Deas from Needham Market give insights into his life there. During Lent he wrote 'I wish you were here because we talk about processing the streets on Good Friday and you would be such a help in beating up people! Did I tell you that I was elected to the Ipswich County Club, the only clerical member till the Bishop of Bury etc. joined and that was after me. I seldom went when at Ipswich, and now, naturally have a craving to go! The subscription is not so big now as I am out of the radius. Thomas and I are taxi-ing on Saturday to attend some musical competition and Thomas has (just) composed a polyphonic Kyrie which his choir boys (and girls) are to sing as one of the items'.

Mrs. F. Brett (who still lives at Needham Market) and her husband lived next-door to Wason's cottage and Fr. Hargrave Thomas brought his new Assistant Priest to their door saying, 'This is Fr. Wason. Would you kindly look after him?' Mrs. Brett remembers him vividly and her observations paint a vivid picture of the Assistant Priest who by then had reached the age of 75. Even at that time he was a heavy smoker, getting through at least 20 Players a day. Mrs. Brett was never allowed to cook for him or do his laundry, but she always made his bed and cleaned for him. By then he had become very thin and rather frail. He was never a very sociable person and had little to say unless he required something. Mrs. Brett observed that he would rarely look anybody straight in the face whilst speaking to them, but always kept his head down. She saw in him a frail and harmless old gentleman, who did not crave for company socially, but was devoted to his Church, which was his life. He rose for Mass every day at 7 a.m., except on one very bad winter's morning, when she found him on her doorstep, with a candle in his hand and dressed only in his pyjamas and red slippers, asking her to 'Tell Padre I'll be late – Overslept'!

He was always to be seen either in a black suit or cassock and biretta. Once when he mislaid his biretta, it was found in his bed. His clerical collars he carefully made himself out of white linen. He spent hours reading the newspaper and always had a rest after lunch, lying on the floor, with a newspaper over his face. Mrs. Brett remembers him holding meetings at his cottage and also possessing a table tennis board, which he lent to the Bretts, but then asked for it back in order to lend it to some soldiers. She said 'He shuffled along, poor old fellow. Nobody really knew him'. He left Needham Market before the Winter of 1943 and it may well have been that Fr. Hargrave Thomas was anxious about his frailty and felt that he should go somewhere where he could be looked after properly. It seems that he went north again, to York, where he was sleeping in All Saints Anker Hold around Easter 1944 and to Mumby, near Alford, Lincs, where he stayed at the Vicarage during the latter part of the year, busily writing.

Mumby St. Thomas was a small village which had become an Anglo-Catholic centre under Fr. William Augustine Mitchell, who was its Vicar from 1918–1962 when, it is said, the Diocesan Authorities asked him to leave because of his great age, making him so furious that he set fire to many of the church papers and documents. He went to live with his daughter in Australia, although his body was brought back for burial in an unmarked grave in Mumby churchyard.

After a quarter of a century 'on the road', Sandys Wason returned to live in London. In 1946 (at the age of 78) the Bishop of London licensed him to officiate at St. Peter's Church, Garford Street, Limehouse, where his friend, Fr. Cyril Hordern, was Vicar. Fr. Hordern found him a room in which to make his home at 50 East India Dock Road, E 14, and was able to pay him the occasional guinea for saying Mass for the small congregation in this Anglo-Catholic Dockland Shrine.

Frank Baker, in the 'Cornish Review' gives a powerful description of the aged Sandys Wason. 'Towards the end of his life, sitting by the fire in his room in the East India Dock Road, with a biretta sliding forward over his white skull, his

fingers fumbling in the pages of his Breviary, his typewritten
sheets of prose and poetry sliding around chair and floor and
sometimes serving to light his cigarette. There, where the
lorries thundered to the Docks and the walls were grimed with
the smoke and dust of East London — Wason was still the
priest, still Perpetual Curate of Curty-with Gunwalloe.

In September 1948 he placed an announcement in the
advertisement columns of the 'Church Times' — 'Venez à
mon Jubilé' (part of the verse in French by Eustache
Deschamps) — announcing in his own inimitable and singular
way the Golden Jubilee of his Ordination to the Priesthood,
which was duly celebrated with style at a Jubilee Mass on
September 25th in St. Peter's at 11 a.m.

Mr. Alan Shadwick, for 31 years on the Editorial Staff of
the Church Times, on a cold Sunday morning in December
1949, took a bus-ride, then a walk, to St. Peter's Limehouse
to find Fr. Wason, having read of him and having had a great
desire to see him. His account gives us a picture of the frail 82
year old priest, who was drawing near to the end of his life,
but was still very much in action. Mr. Shadwick's walk took
him to the Dockyard gates — 'and here at what seemed to be
the world's end, I suddenly perceived a frail old man making
for a little church down a side street. He had combined a
biretta with a nondescript overcoat. One of his turn-ups was
up and the other was down. He walked with a stick. That
would be Sandys Wason, I thought, and Sandys Wason it
was.'

He then described how Wason sang the Mass ('if you could
call it singing — all on one note') for about 15 or 16 poor
people. 'When he came down for the Asperges, he seemed to
have had difficulty with the rose-coloured cope, which was
open down the side instead of at the front. Maybe this
arrangement gave him more freedom to give us a real soaking,
which he proceeded to do with the utmost vigour'. He
mentioned how Wason, his old clothes covered by rich
vestments, was supported by acolytes up the altar steps and
how they had placed an electric fire at the end of the altar 'at
which he sat and warmed his hands while some notices were
read out, a monocle dangling on the rose chasuble'. When, a
few months later, Mr. Shadwick paid a second visit, a lady in

the church told him that Fr. Wason had gone up to Yorkshire for a rest.

He had gone, in fact, to East Haugh, Carleton, near Pontefract. The house still stands, set back up a winding drive, above the road to Darrington – a large, gaunt, rambling and rather forbidding Victorian red-brick house, with a short tower. Its then owner, Mrs. Watts, let out sections of the house as apartments and Wason had several stays there during the 1940s. Frank Baker visited him there in 1947, just before his 80th birthday, when he found his old friend looking better and younger than when he had met him on Euston Station two years before. Mrs. Watts showed Frank Baker a large upstairs room in the house which was empty, its window panes broken and its ceiling blackened by fire. This had been Fr. Wason's room, until he had a rather unfortunate accident with a lighted cigarette, but his miraculously patient landlady explained, 'He was very good. He came and told me it was on fire. The Brigade was most helpful'!

It was to this house that he came in 1950 and spent what were to be his last days. His landlady in Limehouse needed to go for a holiday. He had not been too well for a time and so Daisy Deas arranged for him to go to East Haugh. Here he became weak and ill for a short while and, on July 15th 1950, at the age of 83, he died peacefully, having received the Last Sacraments the previous day. Somebody (possibly Miss Deas) wrote – 'At 10 a.m. there was a swish of angels' wings in the room – and Father Wason smiled and left us'!

Fr. Hordern, writing in St Peter's Limehouse Parish Leaflet, said of him, 'Who would have thought that this simple, kindly and ill-clothed old priest had led the spearhead of the attack on Anglican authority for the Service of Benediction. That a library of some dozen books and the poorest of furniture – barely sufficient to furnish two rooms in the East End of London, were the sole material possessions of him who was related to a former Archbishop and who had mingled freely with the leading writers of his day. It is a cause for pride and thankfulness that we at St. Peter's had the benefit of his ministrations during his last few years'.

The small churchyard of Carleton's little 19th century

church, with its double bell-cot, had long been filled and a small cemetery had been made about a quarter of a mile to the south of the church, along Moor Lane, and it is here that Fr. Wason was laid to rest. The granite cross which marks his grave is now partly obscured from immediate view by a tall conifer planted on the grave. It was not until 1957 that this memorial to him was erected, largely as the result of an appeal in the Church Times, signed by John Betjeman and Compton Mackenzie. In response to this, many small donations came in from brother priests and others who had known him, including Fr. Hordern, who stated his hope that the memorial would be a crucifix and would be inscribed with a couplet from Wason's own writings, also £1 from Daisy Deas' cousin Anne from Scotland, who wrote 'As you know, his religious views and mine were quite at variance, but I know he was a good man'.

The memorial is a granite cross, with a small metal figure of the Crucified. One the base is inscribed

In Memory
LEIGHTON SANDYS WASON
Priest and Poet
Died 15th July 1950
Requiescat in Pace.

Wason's Character and Writings

The story of Fr. Wason's life could be described as one failure after another, yet his achievements have been remembered where many who could be called 'greater than he' have been forgotten. Fr. Walke rightly said of him that 'he blazed a trail'. Having looked at the life of this singular character, who was once described as 'Spare of frame, austere and pale of countenance, with monocle, long cigarette-holder and biretta', we now attempt to gain some insight into his character by looking at what those who knew him had to say about him and by recounting a few more of the 'stories' which have developed around him.

Throughout his life he was unashamedly himself, leaving those who encountered him to either accept him as he was, or to do the other thing!

He certainly was a true eccentric, in the nicest and most correct meaning of the word − he was not one who tried to create an impression of eccentricity, but rather he lived his somewhat unusual life assuming that he was perfectly normal and that it was the rest of the world that was very often 'different'. Frank Baker's description of him in a busy London Bar shows this beautifully − 'Wason immediately settled himself in a chair and concluded Vespers over a glass of Cherry Brandy. I have never seen him to better advantage, nor more divinely oblivious of the sensation he was making'. Another writes of him: 'Fr. Wason had wandered into a world to which he did not belong'. Wason himself once defined an eccentric as one who used an article for a purpose other than that for which it had been intended – and he often lived out this definition!

Fr. Bernard Walke writes that 'There are some people against whom, like children, it would seem impossible to use violence. Father Wason is one of these, for his aristocratic face, like a Chinese carving in ivory, provokes no passion. I think that the men who invaded his house that morning must have closed their eyes, as men about to destroy something very old and rare'. He compares his old friend to the White Knight in 'Through the Looking Glass' – for ever falling off his horse with the setting sun illuminating his white face', also to the mediaeval saint who caused great inconvenience to his Bishop by refusing to be parted from a crucifix and an image of Our Lady, which it was his custom to carry in either hand when he walked abroad – 'so impractical and so aloof from ordinary affairs'.

Fr. Walke tells of their visit, with the artists Ernest and Dod Proctor, to a luncheon party at Cury where, after the very long cycle-ride, they were greeted by a notice on the door, stating 'No-one to enter' – then a vision of Wason rushing in from the garden, cassock tucked up around his waist and arms full of iris blooms, muttering as he passed, 'Colour-scheme of the table all wrong – must get it right for Dod Proctor'. Then, after another wait, Wason shouted from the bedroom window, 'Table all wrong without a black centre. Am looking for my tall hat'. Then after another delay, their host opened the door and greeted them as if they had just arrived. The dining table was adorned with the tall hat filled with flowers as its centrepiece – the product of much trouble and effort as a compliment to his guests.

He tells also of another dinner party given by the Mackenzies, when a last minute telegram was sent to Wason, inviting him also. The answer came back – 'have gone to bed to think out the best way to get to you'. He eventually arrived, very tired and cross that they had already dined without waiting for him, saying, 'I told you that I had gone to bed. It was hardly necessary to say that I might be late'. When asked the obvious question why he had decided to go to bed if he intended coming out to dinner, he replied, 'When I have had

some wine — and you'd better open another bottle of
Champagne — I will explain to you how much easier it is to
think out the kind of problem I was faced with when you are
in bed'!

Even in his early days as a Freshman at Oxford, he missed
a breakfast party, and two days later his host received a
grubby scrap of paper, upon which was smeared, 'Dear T.
Sorry I cannot breakfast with you tomorrow. Excuse coal. No
ink'.

Although he was very much a law unto himself in so many
ways, and must occasionally have been positively insufferable
to his friends, he was in fact the most generous and deep-
feeling person. When he first heard of Fr. Walke's serious
illness, he sent him a telegram: 'Saying Mass for your
intention tomorrow — 10.30 a.m.', followed by another the
following day, saying: 'Too late, overslept — Tomorrow
without fail' and then sent by post a relic of St. Teresa of the
Child Jesus, which was his most treasured possession.

Frank Baker, who actually shared a home with him for a
time, gives glimpses of him 'far into the night, polishing the
line of a sonnet in his armchair by the fire, with all the
impedimenta of his profession — Breviary, Missal, cookery
books, copies of 'The Times', dictionary, ink bottle, typewriter, playing cards, sheets of typing paper, carbons, stray
and scattered chess-men — littered haphazardly on the floor
around his feet'. He remembered Wason upsetting a cup of
coffee over the typewriter balanced on his knees, and when
asked 'How in God's name are we to dry the wretched thing,'
replying tersely 'Put it in the oven, of course' and that is
exactly where it went, as if it was the most natural thing to do.

Fr. Wason loved cooking, especially experimenting, and
was often to be found with his head in a cookery book. He
once gave his guests 'Torrijas', which were fingers of bread,
dusted in sugar, soaked in sherry, fried in butter and then (in
Wason's case) laid out to dry by the fire on sheets of 'The
Times'. Frank Baker described him as 'a tyrant with im-
plements' — standing over the stove and shouting through to
him to serve him with things — forks, slices, graters, whisks,
egg-cups, cloves, cinnamon, chives, etc.

Above all, Fr. Wason was first and foremost a priest of the

Church Catholic, with very decided views which he could not really bring himself to believe that everybody else did not automatically accept. And he made his views known, like his utter detestation of the Prayer Book. Once in the pulpit he held up a copy, and then announced 'This is the Book of Comic Prayer, and this is where it is going' and then cast it violently to the floor.

Many people found him to be a totally impassive person, with very little expression in his face or in his voice, and his style of conducting services reflected this. When saying Mass his speech was little more than a mutter, which was almost toally inaudible, even in the parts where it was meant to be heard. He found it impossible to sing the Mass in tune. His sermons were often very short (usually no more than three or four minutes) and invariably they ended abruptly. He read with the aid of a monocle and people remember this integral part of the Wason attire dangling on its black cord in front of him as he conducted the service. Invariably his biretta sat firmly upon the top (but never perched on the back) of his head, wherever he was and whatever he was doing. Occasionally he was clad in his cassock but usually, rather than being clothed in 'clerical black' as we would expect in a priest of his persuasion, he wore the most amazingly shabby and un-coordinate attire – but always topped off by the biretta!

At the centre of his life and his routine was the offering of the Holy Sacrifice of the Mass and the recitation of the round of Daily Offices (not Morning and Evening Prayer from the Book of Common Prayer but the full round of Offices from the Roman Breviary). The story of Walke and Wason crossing the central gangway of the stalls at a London Theatre, Wason genuflecting to the stage and repeating the action on the way back from the bar at the interval, Walke observing 'You've no need to genuflect, you're not at Mass' and Wason replying 'Everything's Mass to me', has a deep significance because that, in short, *was* Wason. His central duty as a priest was to be at the Altar – this was the best way he knew of praying for people and for making things happen, to offer the Holy Sacrifice for a particular person or intention, and always on Sundays for those 'stupid people' who had refused his prayers and ministrations at Cury. And this was not because of any false virtue or persecution complex, but because to him he was still their priest and therefore it was his bounden duty before God to serve them in this way.

Frank Baker, when he occasionally served for him, would hear him mutter as they made their way from the vestry to the Altar 'Anyone there?' Often on a weekday Mass the answer would be 'no', and then the reply would be 'Good. Latin Mass' – and then 'Introibo ad altare Deo' and Fr. Wason's umpteenth hundredth Mass would begin in the way that he considered nearest to perfection.

The Sacrament of Reconciliation was of great importance to Wason, but it is accounts of his great need to receive this sacrament, rather than of Wason the Confessor, that we hear. He and Bernard Walke attended a Diocesan Conference at Truro and at the Eucharist on the last morning Walke said to him, 'You must receive Communion this morning'. 'I can't' was the reply. 'Why?' 'Because I have sinned'. 'Sinned?' said Walke. 'You went to Confession yesterday'. 'I've sinned since yesterday', was the reply. In the cathedral, Walke took his place near the Altar, whilst Wason went to the back, until just before the Consecration, when Walke heard his friend making for him, overturning a chair on the way. He knelt down beside Bernard and said, 'Ber, hear my Confession'. 'I can't' said Walke 'It's too late. Go away'. And Wason wandered back to his place, muttering, 'Too late, too late'.

Fr. Jolly of St. Enoder remembers Wason rather rudely correcting him once at the tea-table for mispronouncing the word 'timbre'. Afterwards however Wason humbly asked if Fr. Jolly would hear his Confession 'which I did with puzzlement as to why he should ask me when there were other better priests available'. Mother Teresa tells of Wason's reply to Walke, when told that just about all the farmers who had helped to throw him out of Cury had been visited by some serious misfortune. His comment was 'It is interesting to see how the wicked, myself included, have been punished'.

The Breviary contains all that is needed to recite the eight divine Offices which punctuated each day for Roman Catholic priests and of course Wason took this discipline very seriously indeed. His copy of the Breviary was always with him and he could be found with his head buried in it when he visited friends, went out to the Pub for a drink, rode his bicycle through the Cornish lanes, sat in his London book-shop oblivious of customers, or even during a church service when everybody else was singing Evensong! Occasionally the book was discovered to be upside-down in his hands; some-times he would be reading a morning Office in the afternoon, or vice-versa and in emergencies he might say several Offices, one after the other, in order to catch up! Frank Baker writes: 'Whatever he may be doing, he will at some period of the day sink back into the Breviary, his fingers beginning auto-matically to fumble and probe into the pages of the ancient black book while he talks to you and grows more absent. I have never known him, however eager he might be about some other work, to forget the Office'.

Yet the people to whom he ministered at Cury and Gunwalloe, also those in his later travels, found him far from aloof. He often referred in letters to the 'lambs' he gathered around him in parishes where he worked, or to his 'buddies' from the churches who would be invited to his home to eat, or to play chess, cards, or table-tennis with him.

Perhaps it is the words of Frank Baker, remembering the last time that he saw Wason, then aged 80, late at night at East Haugh, which best encapsulate him –

'But all the time I was studying the head bent over the Breviary, the fingers enclosing between the leaves photographs of friends, living and dead. Tomorrow morning, I told myself, he would probably say Mass and I wished very much that I could be there to serve that Mass as I had done in earlier days. Dark winter mornings in Hedsor Church came into my mind; hands moving slowly in the ancient Mysteries. This is as I best remember Wason, the priest withdrawing into the secret, silent world of the Holy Mass, unlocking a door which he alone seems able to enter, yet leaving it sufficiently open for us to see something of the light inside. For Fr. Wason remains above all things and is in all his activities, a priest of God, whose true religious sense and devotion has defeated the clumsy tricks of time and enshrined the ordinary pursuits of life on the eternal altar of sacrifice'.

As a postscript to all of this – how very fitting that Frank

Baker should have had cause to write in a letter to Daisy Deas, dated April 26th 1951 – 'You could not have sent me a more precious relic than the monocle and the pencil. As for the cigarette case, I don't recall him using it, but anything that he handled is a treasure'.

Sandys Wason will be remembered (by those who have managed to discover some of them) for his writings in poetry and prose. It is interesting that this man who led a singular and lonely life in many ways, who was poorly treated and largely unrecognised by the Establishment in the Church and who often lived pretty near to the poverty line, has also been described by no less a person than the late Poet Laureate, Sir John Betjeman as 'the greatest living master of nonsense verse' in his day.

Wason's literary talent was considerable and he enjoyed writing throughout his life. His skill with the pen began to flourish during his undergraduate days at Oxford, where he edited 'The Spirit Lamp', which published twelve issues, up to 1893. His successor as Editor was Lord Alfred Douglas.

Wherever he was residing, his old battered Remington typewriter was near and handy, usually equipped with an over-used and faded ribbon. He was often surrounded by mountains of papers, with handwritten and typewritten verses scattered everywhere, and particularly on the floor around where he was sitting. He would spend hour after hour poring over some paragraph or poem which he had created – crossing bits out, writing in alternative or better phrases, altering, adjusting, altering again and then coming back to the same piece of work after months or years having mislaid it! Rarely did he feel that one of his works was finished, or rather perfected, to his satisfaction. 'If only I could leave one good line', he would say, whilst musing over a crumpled manuscript from a pile of incomplete writings, which may also have served the purpose of being used to clutch the odd lump of coal from his scuttle!

His output of limericks was immense, but few were ever published, or in his eyes anywhere near ready for publication – and many of them were complete nonsense at its most ridiculous and glorious. In the 1940s he did assemble some 40 or so for publication, but no book ever materialized. Frank Baker particularly liked

The noted Bon Vivant, John Jubb
(Connoisseur of sound wine and safe grub),
Affixes on spikes the chops he dislikes
Outside the Conservative Club.

John Jubb, who had been a Roman Catholic priest, was latterly priest-in-charge of Baldersby S. James, near Ripon. He wrote in an article intended for the Cornish Review that to him the King of Nonsense was Baron Von Munchausen. His one collection of Nonsense Verse was published by Max Groschen in 1913 and entitled 'Magenta Minutes', from one poem in it, which is probably the best known and most quoted of all his secular verse. It is entitled 'Kabale und Liebe' and it begins

Many a mad magenta minute
Lights the lavender of life;
Keran-happuch at her spinet
Psalms the scarlet song of strife.
Keran-happuch is my wife.

Whilst at Cury, Wason was a magnet for literary personalities, who came to see him and his near neighbour Charles Turley Smith, including people like Conan Doyle. It is interesting that he did not need to travel all over the country in order to creep after them — they came to him. He was clearly much respected in the literary world.

In 1927, Cope & Fenwick published Wason's novel, 'Palafox', which describes the adventures of a young man who acquired a small metal convex disc, which gave him the power to read the secret thoughts of other people. The dust-jacket was designed by the artist Gladys Hynes and the Introduction was written by Compton Mackenzie, who gives a sensitive insight into his friend's character and skill at writing, calling him 'the author of some of the most exquisite Nonsense Verse in the English Language'. He concludes by telling the reader that once when the author came to stay with him in Hampshire — 'He arrived with two shirts, a tooth-brush and an immense turbot, an absolutely immense turbot. And just as I enjoyed eating that turbot, I have enjoyed reading this book'. Before the 'Contents' page is a short introduction by the Author, beginning 'Dear Public. Sometime ago I was deprived of a fat and important living in Cornwall for holding an illegal service. I am advised by two experts in Ecclesiastical Law that in their considered opinion there is positively nothing illegal in this tale'.

A fascinating booklet, which appeared in the years following his removal from Cury, was published by the Society of SS. Peter and Paul, entitled 'The Anathema Alphabet, or Syllabus of Errors condemned by the English Bishops since 1840. Compiled by Sandys Wason, Perpetual Curate of Cury-with-Gunwalloe, Cornwall. With a Foreword by "Tractarian"'. It would be interesting to know who 'Tractarian' was, because the style of writing, bitter irony and dry wit in the opening 'Foreword and Appeal' is so typical of Wason himself. There then follows 'A list of Articles, Doctrines, Ceremonies and matters of Discipline condemned by one or other of the Bishops of Ecclesia Anglicana from 1840 to 1920', arranged alphabetically. Beginning with 'Apocrypha, Abbeys, Abbots and Abbesses, assistant Priests, Acolytes ...' continuing through 'Christmas Carols, Catafalques, Cultus of the Sacred Heart, Our Lady and St. Joseph, Cultus of King Charles the First, Minor Cults, Celibacy' and 'Octaves, Ombrellinos, Oxen in Cribs, Oblations ...' it ends with 'Yule, Yuletide and Yule Carols, Yearly Confession and the Use of York' and finally, under 'Z', the single word 'Zeal'. Six pages at the end give details of the Episcopal condemnation of some of the items mentioned, including ablutions, banners and clerical beards! Reading this little collection of words, one could easily become convinced that if the English Bishops of the period had got their way, there would be little if any religion left in the Church of England!

In 1948 a little book of poems, entitled 'Simon Dean and Other Poems' was published by Elkin Mathews of Cork Street, London. It contains a long poem about a lad called Simon Dean and the Mass and ten shorter poems, ending with 'All Souls Day, Gunwalloe, 1913' which portrays the dignity and meaning of his annual service by the sea, and concludes:-

'Tis for no dancing, this our fine array.
The frankincense, the flowers we seaward fling
Are to no Neptune flung; for him we sound
No music magical this All Souls Day.
In our Atonement, our peace-offering,
Devoted by the living to the drowned.

Two years earlier, Wason had collaborated with his friend from undergraduate days, Sir Herbert Grierson, in producing 'The Personal Note', which was published by Chatto & Windus. He once remarked about it: 'My idea, but Grierson did all the work'. Being a Wason idea, we can expect it to be just a little out of the ordinary – and it was. It was an anthology of Prefaces to a whole variety of books, which made rather novel reading, especially for those who tend to skip these when reading the book proper. When the book came out, Wason distributed copies of his visiting card to various people, with 'Presentation of this card entitles the bearer to one copy of "The Personal Note". S.W.' in his handwriting on the back of the card.

Several of his writings and poems which were never published exist, and more are being discovered. There is his treatise on Benediction, intended for publication by Cope & Fenwick (c. 1917), which survives in part. The ill-fated novel 'Storm in an Egg-Cup', one manuscript of which went to America for hopeful publication and never returned and the other disappeared for ever amongst Newport's wartime salvage, would have made fascinating reading had it been published. Then there was 'Phoenix – the new Catholic Review to end all Catholic Reviews' – with Wason as sole proprietor. This was to rule both his and Frank Baker's lives for a time, but again it never actually got off the ground.

This was when Frank Baker was organist at Hedsor, Bucks and was living at the vicarage there. Wason came to stay for three weeks, armed with 'innumerable addresses, notebooks, printers' estimates, specimen types and the battered, ash-ridden Remington'. 'Must get T.S. Eliot' he said as he entered – then briefly to the Vicar in whose home he was to stay "Well, Father? Any converts?". 'And Wodehouse' he continued, 'Must get them together for the first number'. For three weeks he and Baker wrote hundreds of letters to Anglo-Catholic clergy in England and the Colonies – and also to Queen Mary – requesting subscriptions in advance!

Literary friends and contacts were invited to submit articles, many of which were returned by Wason with adverse criticisms. He read them and muttered, 'How can they write such drivel'! He went down to Nashdom Abbey to sell the idea of 'Phoenix' to the Abbot and to Dom Gregory Dix. He even planned an advertising slot which was to use professional actors and singers performing on the back of a lorry. But support was not forthcoming; both Fr. Walke and Filson Young (the BBC producer of the St. Hilary broadcasts) warned Frank against the idea. Wason's enthusiasm waned and the idea of 'Phoenix' was buried, *not* to rise again!

His poems appeared occasionally in anthologies, including 'The Penguin Book of Comic Verse', 'The Nonsensibus' by Wyndham Lewis and 'Altar and Pew' by John Betjeman, also in the occasional Parish Magazine, including the Graham Street Quarterly and Hedsor Parish Magazine.

He wrote (almost certainly whilst at Mumby) a series of articles for the Parish Magazine of Winthorpe, near Skegness, in early 1945, entitled 'The Religion of a Lonely Old Man'. In this series, the villagers were given Papalist teaching about the present state of the Church of England, and juicy material like 'Ways and means of exterminating the matricide called the Reformation', also 'The South India Scheme, long ago considered as dead and cold as mutton, is once again alive and frisking as formidably as a Spring lamb'. He suggests that the Church of England might have its wings righteously clipped if lay-folk were to take positive action – parents and God-parents insisting that their children should be confirmed with the use of Chrism Oil, payment of the Diocesan Quota should be discontinued, attendance at cathedrals except for weddings and funerals should cease – and then Bishops would be forced to abandon the South India Scheme. He further suggests 'Also the Roman Missal in English on Sundays and weekdays must be introduced Sunday next'!

His poems and prose (corrected and re-drafted many times) give great pleasure to the reader, but more fascinating still are the personal letters that he wrote. These were written intuitively and are honest mirrors into his thought and character. They have not been edited, revised or corrected for a reading public but are personal.

There even exists a Christmas Card sent by Fr. Wason to a friend and this is a little gem of Wasonic handling. It is a silly card and not the sort that he would have chosen to select. On the front is a cat, riding a toy horse and sitting upon a load of parcels, with the message 'Wishing you a load of happiness for Christmas'. Inside in pencil is Wason's personal message to its recipient:-

> No true cards here, hence
> I interrupt this as
> the Black King
> riding into Bethlehem
> laden with presents
> on the Palm Sunday ass.
> With love
> Ora pro
> Sandys Wason.

A selection of Fr. Wason's poems, together with a short, readable and informative Memoir of him, written with great love and feeling by Fr. Cyril Calveley Hordern, was published in 1979. Copies of this booklet are still obtainable.

The extracts from letters which follow were written mostly to Daisy Deas. Although personal, these are worth sharing with all Wason enthusiasts. The sections quoted are exactly as he wrote and punctuated them. This includes his use of the small 'i' when used as a pronoun referring to himself. Whether this simply saved him trouble, or was an eccentric affectation, or more likely a reflection of the very real and self-effacing humility which he possessed, we do not know.

Saturday. The Poplars, Swainby. c.1936 – to Daisy Deas).

Algy hopes to be down on Monday – I hope he won't overtax his strength & get a relapse. This means, I suppose that I shall be leaving in say 2 Sundays, next (tomorrow) and another. Potto is unspeakably charming. I have now been

here since I wrote & I've seen no one except the sick people —
weekly Communicants — though Mrs. Barker is always
asking me to use her car (When I leave I want to stay a night
in York — but, if Banister is still bad I expect the Anchor
Hold will be occupied). I expect Mrs. B. has told you that her
old servcant fell through the kitchen table & has been
unconscious ever since. These Louie & others I haven't seen.
I can't worry her — perhaps she will take me as I feel, as ever,
a little shy in bursting in on crowds of strange
people ....

Can you find out from your taxi-man what he would charge
to take me round York for some hours if I come in on
Saturday so that I might go and see some of our lambs? The
trousers are heavenly, thank you for having them done. I
force myself to take a small walk on my lonesome, but I miss
our walks to the Club and my club and the weird Chapel! —
and it's the same at Newport — but the view from my window
keeps me going — if I don't get out much.

I suppose the Pope never takes any exercise. I wanted to get
over to Pickering to see an old priest Fr Bryan there and to
Goathland to see a lamb I used to see in hospital. Mrs. Barker
as always made nothing of the vast distances but I felt both
were too far off. How I envy the Pope his car! What a growler
I am, aren't I? It is merely the background thought of my
scrmons to come tomorrow I think, that keeps me so gloomy.

I do devour The Times — I can't think why you don't make
the Pope take it in. There is some substance in it. Newport
keeps calm & sane & the same. I heard from Cottrell, the Saint
and Mrs. Wilkinson — all here is normal — how *horrible* &
fearful & ghastly & impossible normality is! — so complacent
— and here I am grousing again so I'd better leave off, before
the pen refuses to write.

Yours always with love to you & the Pope & Digger & the
unforgotten lambs.

S. Titus 1936 (from Swainby — To Daisy Deas.)

My letters must be getting a bit boring!
(Please give Albert's letter to Pat. You'll see he *says* he'll go
to Mass (?). In case you have forgotten he has a squint and a

squashed face – but you never forget anyone – a royal memory is yours). Talking of Mass, I don't think I shall come to this Mass on Tuesday. It's in the dinner hour and the only chance I shall have of seeing anyone. Algy is in fine fettle and Francisca – I must call her something & I haven't tumbled to her Christian name yet – as Franciscan as ever ....

By the way, you don't say where I was to stay the night. It is cold wherever I stay nowadays – Anchor Hold or lodgings – although the bedrooms are so full of ghastly and no doubt expensive furniture that one can't breathe, sheets are never provided – linen sheets I mean. If ever my dream legacy crawls in, I hope to treat myself in my new house to a pair of Simon Pure .... I wonder if coffee will be served on Tuesday, for if Silas Harris turns up, there will be at least two bêtes noires at table. I should like to ask you out to lunch but Pat would have a fit. I hope there will be a 'good number' (Algy seems a bit great on numbers and I try and persuade him that the church is packed. I still tell her she coddles the people – but my weighty words don't somehow seem to sink in as they should). I went to Dott (S. John's Stockton) to Confession. I like him, he is so peacable although he has a car (I suppose Pat never goes anywhere nowadays with his. I hope he walks sometimes) .... Everything but the meat here is all right. It would be a relief to eat a porterhouse steak – especially as I have never eaten one. I expect you have often enough, part of one as I believe is enough for three or four people. Mrs. Saunderson gives me of her honey which is very good. I hope you aren't starving yourself & feeding Digger on sweetbreads and ortolans ....

(Dated 1936 – possibly to Fr. Shaw.)

Please tell your York Intelligence Department that I hope to go out to supper tonight with one of the Wardens and that they are welcome to use the item (gratis) in the Gossip Columns of the All Hallows' Invigilator. I have been obliged, very reluctantly, to write to your Editress contradicting the report that I was to stay at York on Monday and pointing out that though the *place*, York, was absolutely correct, the proposed *date* was Saturday not Monday and that the length of sojourn was undoubtedly wrong as my time-table here, enclosed to her, undoubtably proves ...... Rightly or wrongly the Public considers my movements of pressing importance; it follows them like the dogs at Wembley Dogodrome. Hence any inaccuracy is likely to be fraught with super-annoyance and irritability, hence, I had to contradict your Paper although valuable time had elapsed.

The only question in my mind is whether the Editress will publish my long and interesting letter of contradiction. I flatter myself that she will because any signed letter of mine is (practically) worth its weight in dollars. O.P.M. Sandys Wason.

(To Daisy Deas, from La Chaise, Newport).

.... Whitby has printed one of my worst poems in his Graham Street Quarterly. The other verses are still in London waiting a credulous publisher. i am hoping to buckle-to over my Egg story when i get to Mevagissey, did i tell you of my birthday party? if not i will, also of the Buckmasters golden wedding. It's pouring with rain tonight; i don't expect the buddies will turn up as evensong must be well over by now. La Chaise is peaceful tonight, only the ticking of the alarum clock. i find that i have been making omelettes all wrong all my life. The secret is to heat the pan empty pan, so that when you put in the butter the butter nearly catches fire. You then in a couple of seconds make the omelette off the fire in the heat of the pan only. This is from Boulestin's book 'What shall we have today?'. Frank Baker ex-organist of S. Hilary has been staying here, Monday till Friday and in that time wrote a short novel! Wonderful facility isn't it and the novel is astonishing to say quite readable ...... i enclose the parish paper of Hedsor where Frank Baker is now organist as the Rector has printed one of my poems the one i like best of all. Wants another for Easter. i've told him i have one on that mystery but that i had a Scotch grandmother and that therefore, i must ask half a guinea for it. i don't mind occasionally giving a poem but as a practice – mean isn't it? particularly as they are a drug in the market!

(To Daisy Deas, dated Feast of S. Denis 1937).

Your long letter was most grateful and comforting. In the middle of lunch at the Cottrells i had a spot of wind, had forgotten i had a touch before, had to lie down. Brandy was brought and i was all right again in a quarter of an hour . . . . . . Very few at church . . . . . A terrible wouldbe simple appealling (sic) sermon here from a vicar at Roath, the veriest garbage.

I have taken a locum at Tillbrook, Hunts. Dallas is rector there. i may do a spot of writing and go on from there, only twelve days, to Hedsor . . . . . . There's a horse running today called Palafox . . . . . . Pat sent two halfpenny envelopes one to you and one to me with nothing whatever inside them. i wonder what they were supposed to have. Your beans were delicious also your ham. i attack your prawns this afternoon, Friday for lunch. The weather still keeps heavenly. i wonder how the cyst is going. the fourth Magus over the mantel is still a joy to me . . . . . I am getting back-bound at the type-writer so u forgive me if i stop. i expect Pat got this job for me. Dallas of Tillbrook never said a word to me about it. It will be most frightfully dull there. He complained that he had had no holiday for two years. Father Wainwright never took a holiday all the years he was at S.P's London Docks.

(To Daisy Deas, from 11 King William Street, Needham Market).

Never a line about your accident; do write when you're in the mood and have time. The church must look pretty awful without the lovely windows. I wish you were here because we talk about processing the streets on Good Friday and you would be such a help in beating up people. There are lovely walks here, fields and small streams and old churches. i said Mass for you and Pat the other day . . . . . . i had a letter from Silas Harris yesterday; he is well of his 'flu and writes more cheerfully than usual. He thinks the *new* vicar of East Markham is some kind of Anglo-catholic but hasn't called on him yet. Also please tell Pat that X Southwell is rumoured to have insisted on making some young men who asked him for leave to Reserve, doing it in an aumbry and doing away with the tabernacle and reserving in both kinds. In return for these bits of news, please tell me how S. Samson's and the other church near All SS is getting on. i forget the name .... (trying the ribbon). Endless practices there which i attend. i suppose the daily practice of the choir still goes on at All Saints, how far away it sounds. A lot of alert the other night, not very far from here. i had to stop typing as the amiable but very energetic Watchers would have butted in, bless them ...... Vicar still keen on going out in the streets and perhaps pubs on Good Friday. His daughter Elizabeth, the second one is a nurse or probationer at Addenbrook's Cambridge, is coming in the taxi to Stowmarket. Love and oremus pro nobis invicem, always sandys wason. Write when in the mood; your letters are a great resource.

(To Daisy Deas, from Needham Market).

You are a wonder! i mean knowing so exactly how Satan and his angels plan things. You also say *i* have no safeguard against them; i can't think how you can tell this. Altogether your welcome letter is full of mysteries. S.Y.A. is the vii years association, binding all its members, all are laics, to the precepts of the church. Denys Hawe used to run it and meetings were held in the Anchor Hold. Apparently the York S.Y.A. station, according to their paper called Platform, has gone bust. Thank you for the news of the water-spout. What of the dear Barkers and their postulant for the priesthood, Cyril Collins?

Thank you so much about the bird; i may ask a chaplain called Tuesday of all curious names to share it with me but if cooked here over the parlour fire (there is but one fire) it will have to be spatch-cocked and i've never tried this way of cooking a bird and how to do gravy and bread sauce on the fire at the same time also puzzles me; my good daily-maid would no doubt offer to cook it for me but she only uses her oven occasionally. i always marvelled how you managed to give us such exciting meals under like difficulties. i have solved the problem! there's a bake-house near by and i've seen

buddies taking what was evidently sunday dinners home. i must get Hargrave to come. i am always asking him but he is always due to a meal at home . . . .
i know you love giving things, so will you send me this bird, whatever you will. i have "arranged" to give Father Tuesday and vicar here lunch on Shrove Tuesday which seems an appropriate day? Please do not cook it, beforehand . . . .
i am well and happy here but hope to take another house as soon as ever one falls vacant as this one is shut in by houses and has no garden . . . . . . How are your pets? well, i hope and also that you do not give them all your rations to eat. i wish i had something to send you but till the fine weather comes, i do not go into Ipswich, nine miles, to see and get things. Love and oremus pro invicem.

(To Fr. Peter Blagdon-Gamlen, from 50 East India Dock Road, in very shaky and difficult-to-read handwriting, with many crossings-out.)

Has it occured to you to make a list of *Catholics* in *any* ruri-deanery you like to choose. You would then open your eyes to the fact that we in infinitesimal number. These Aves make no simple clear appeal to outsiders. They are not house plants – and full of names – who cares whether Father Johnson Damian Cantankeros carried a banner of Saint Videntiana. They merely put off people from the Father. Con amore. Sandys Wason.

The Parish Church of St. Corentin, Cury. From an old post-card.

Close up of an early All Soul's Day procession at Gunwalloe. Fr. Bernard Walke is the thurifer (right) and Fr. Wason enters 'stage-left'.

Father Wason dressed for tennis, complete with biretta!

Leighton Sandys Wason

Fr. Wason (right), stands beside his friend, Fr. Patrick Shaw (centre) at York.

Parish Church of St. Corentin, Cury, 1993.

Gunwalloe Church, showing the Poldhu Hotel and the long-demolished pylons of Marconi's Wireless Station in the distance.

Gunwalloe Church in its splendid setting, 1993.

The former Vicarage at Cury, 1993

The former Vicarage at St. Hilary, where the homeless Wason and all his worldly possessions arrived in 1919.

The Oratory Chapel, set up in a room at Cury Vicarage, where Fr. Wason continued his ministry as 'the lawful parish priest'.

All Soul's Day at Gunwalloe.

Scenes at two different All Soul's Day services at Gunwalloe.

All Souls' Day at Gummludo

Outside All Saints, North Street, York with Miss Daisy Deas.

At St. Hilary, with Mrs Annie Walke looking on.

Part Two

My thanks are due to the Editors of the Saturday Review and the Graphic for permission to reprint some of these poems.

Simon Dean

From the square crown upon its granite tower
Down to its granite roots below the vaults
Daft Simon knew Saint Lazarus, root and flower,
Daft Simon knew its beauties and its faults,
Daft Simon knew Saint Lazarus, every stone,
Flesh of his flesh it was, bone of his bone.

Simon had seen his old playmates draw near
And take the Sacred Host; and Simon tried
To learn the Acts of Love and Hope and Fear,
And why "they" let good Christ be crucified.
Simon might blow and serve and cense and ring
But Simon might not eat the Holy Thing.

Simon was "much too young to take the Host.
He must have patience. Patience was the Fruit,
One of the twelve fruits of the Holy Ghost."
And Simon folded up his Sunday suit,
And prayed that he might find the Holy Tree
And taste the fruit, all ate, alas! but he.

"Father, I'm old enough, I've waited long,
Just as you told me. I know Him so well.
I talk to Him; He answers me. I'm strong
Enough to hold Him? And my scaring-bell
Rings Him down every day for you,' he said.
"Not yet awhile," was all the word he had.

And now the priest grew very old and died.
And on his death-bed sent for Simon, who
Ran to the summons, flushed and eager-eyed.
"I sent for you," he said, "to know if you
Had anything to ask before I went,
Where you can ask me nothing." Simon bent

And held his breath a minute while he thought.
"There is one Thing I'd dearly long to have,
The Holy Thing you said I did not ought

To have, not yet awhile," he said. "God save
Your grammar, boy! Well, run and get my pen,
It's on the table in the window. When

"The Requiem for me is over, and
The Absolutions at the catafalque,
And after the new priest's thanksgiving, hand
This letter to him. Don't begin to talk,
Until he's read my letter," said the priest,
"And keep it clean, and don't let it be creased."

He wrapped it in the crimson sash he wore
At Expositions of the Sacrament,
And laid it up upon a shelf before
A picture of the Holy Face. He meant
It should be neither touched, nor even seen,
By any one excepting Simon Dean.

It was the John the Baptist of his soul,
His Jacob ladder and his household god,
His Burning Bush and his Ezekiel roll,
Aladdin Lamp and Ring and Moses' rod.
And Hope and Life and Promise and Content
And heart and eyes and soul and Sacrament.

Between the altar and the chancel-gate,
The body of the father clothed in white
And purple and fine linen lay in state
Upon a velvet bier and drank the light
Of candle-flames unable to disperse
The darknesses which lay beyond the herse.

The Reverend Mother of the Sisterhood
He'd shepherded for over forty years
Was trying hard to pray, do what she would
She could not stay the fountain of her tears
Or clear away the heavy cloud of doubt
Which lay upon her spirit while she thought:

"I hate to hear the babies he was fond of

Exclaim 'They've shut him in a velvet box,'
For children seem to know ... things we despond of.
It's just the very children, still in socks,
Whose souls one positively sees sometimes
Incarnate in their eyes, who hear the chimes

"Of wild anemone or convent crocus
Who face the Crib with small, fat, folded hands,
And seeing eyes, to whom our hocus-pocus
About the soul 'flown off to far-off lands'
Are unbelievable and 'grown-up' fancies,
Like Tidying up one's toys, or Washing Hands is."

And as the Reverend Mother hesitated,
She heard the Angelus begin to ring;
And doubts redoubled rather than abated.
"What does it mean?" she thought. "Just anything
One wants to make it mean. It's so removed
From real life, a fairy tale unproved.

"And nobody, except at Christmas time,
Believes in Bethlehem ... and Nazareth,
It's more than wonderful, of course, sublime.
But true, like motherhood or hate or death?
And if it isn't true, what is the use
Of making out it is? There's some excuse

"For people born and bred up in it all."
And then she saw a shadow in the gloom
Beyond the Rood and heard a sure foot-fall
And saw a laden figure slowly come
And kneel before the overhanging Pyx,
A blind old woman with a frail of sticks.

Who crossed herself and knelt with arms out-stretched
And moved her lips while tears came raining down
Her shrunken cheeks, and soon as if refreshed
Got up again and smoothed her speckled gown
And crossed herself once more and slung her pack
And went upon her way, still turning back

From time to time. The Reverend Mother cried,
And, taking out her rosary, began
To sound the mystery she had denied,
And said another prayer for Father Jan,
And trimmed a taper which began to burn
And sent to tell the boys to take their turn.

For, though "The priest was much too old and slow"
When he was still alive, when he was dead,
"There's none could preach or shrive, as we allow
From Lizard to Penzance or Gurnard's Head,
As our old Father there, a kingly man,"
And all the village watched for Father Jan.

And Simon was to watch at twelve o'clock,
With Jimmie Bray. And he was peacock-proud,
Was Simon, when he heard a Sister knock
Upon the door, and Simon blushed and bowed,
And ran away to fetch his book of prayers,
And then his mother heard a cry upstairs.

And as she heard it Simon Dean had leapt,
Straight from the landing to the room below,
Into her frightened arms and clung and wept,
As if a stake were being driven through
His heart. "My sash, my crimson sash is gone;
I saw it on the shelf this afternoon

"When I came home from school," he moaned. "If you
Are really mazed about my handkerchief,
Good Jesus Christ, do keep it always, do.
We shouldn't think of bothering to search if
You feel you really want it in the least,
But do give back my letter for the priest.

"It can't do You a particle of good.
Do give it back again, I beg and pray,
Or I can never have the Holy Food,
And if You haven't taken it away,
Please make the Devil put it back himself,
Under Your coloured picture on the shelf."

"Now, Simon, time to go," his mother said.
"Run upalong and call for Jimmie Bray.
Twill take some time to get him from the bed
And when you'm there, be sure and make 'm pray.
And don't you go upsetting of yourself,
I'll seek for sash, it may be under shelf."

They knelt down by the catafalque and prayed
And then began to doze off in the heat
And woke up with a start. The sound that made
Them start was gentle, like the sound of wheat
Athwart a wind or bulrushes in thrall
To some clear leat or wayside waterfall.

They saw a priest come through the vestry-door,
(A chalice at his breast), they watched him cross
The dull-trod marbles of the chancel-floor
And both, unfrightened, yet were at a loss
To see a priest they knew but did not know,
And Jimmie whispered Simon, "Let us go."

He spread the corporal and ranged the burse
And, opening out the missal on its rest
Came down again and, stood behind the herse,
He touched his forehead first and then his breast,
And, in his purple chasuble and stole,
Began a mass for his departed soul!

The mass went on: he bowed or genuflected
Or prayed with folded hands or hands upraised,
Just how and when and where the Books directed.
It was a mass Gavantus might have praised!
And Simon blanched when Jimmie stole away,
And set his teeth and forced himself to pray.

"There's something strange about this evening mass,"
Said Simon to himself, "and something solemn,
I'd like to run away like Jimmie has,
But Simon Stylights died upon his column,
And if it's Father Jan, I 'spect he'd know
And wouldn't like me going halfway through."

But, presently, when Simon saw he knew
The mazes of the mass, as forest bees
Know and return upon the way they flew,
He felt his trouble die into a peace
And, recognising mass, his soul had rest
And lay a babe upon its mother's breast.

And wiped away his tears and spoke the Latin
And hardly felt surprised when he turned round,
And, holding up a Host above the paten
Came down the altar-steps without a sound
And placed It in his mouth and disappeared.
He felt as though a tender hand had cleared

The trouble from his brain. "It is the Christ,
It is the good God, Jesus Christ!" he said.
"He didn't want my letter to the priest.
It is a pity Father Jan is dead.
He would have been so proud to hear me say
The Acts I never knew before to-day."

The Lepers' Christmas

Theirs is a dance of death,
　　The dance they dance beneath,
　　　　The Christmas wreath.

Theirs is a bread of tears
Broken; and in their ears
　　　A sound of fears.

Theirs is a wine of pain,
　　The draught they have to drain,
　　　　Time and again.

Yet theirs to rend the veil
Which hides the heavenly Grail,
　　　The manna pale.

Theirs is the blood-red wine
That did incarnadine
　　　The Living Vine.

And theirs to touch the calm
Of a Babe's open palm.
　　　And breathe the balm

Of the one Sharon Rose
Who did for them unclose
　　　Amid the snows,

Of the one Babe Who is
Swift to return with His
　　　The leper's kiss.

Epiphany (2)

The tent was dark, the fended flame
In Mary's lamp was low,
As from the East the wise men came,
Across the snow.

The camels knelt before the Babe;
The magians outspread
The hoarded homages of kings,
Before His bed.

His baby hands strayed o'er the gold;
Upon the myrrh did cling;
Amid the grains of frankincense
Groped wondering.

The tent was dark, the fended flame
In Mary's lamp was low,
As, to the East, the kings returned
Across the snow.

The Forty Martyrs

Before Sebaste, naked on the ice,
The Forty from the Thundering Legion lay.
The cold was on them; closing as a vice
Closes, uncloses, closes to the play
Of some demented Titan, as a sword
Which slays and passes, but to make return
And slay, a wind from Caucasus had bored
Their bodies to the bone. Couched in the fern,
A Roman Guard took frozen sheltering
Or leaped and wrestled fiercely, to aby
A cold so stark no furs no weltering
No blasphemies no bodies could defy.
Like moiling beasts, revolving eyes aflame
With leaping lecheries, the Thermae steamed,
Like mandrakes pent and dancing with the shame
Of prison-glass, they boiled and hissed and screamed.

But Melithon's mother, rigid as the reed
Whereby she stood, and with the resolute
Detachment of a spirit who is freed
From flesh, and with his fixed gaze and mute
As Mary at the Cross before her Son,
A heart, an Anguish and anon a Prayer,
Begun and ended and again begun
With Melithon, to hang and hover there
Where he among the martyrs lain heart-sick
To take what starveling comfort, what faint heat
His flesh might burrow there clave like the wick
Of those coiled human trindles waste with sweat
Of deathly cold, made moan within herself —

> "Pillar of Cloud, make dim
> The Thermae luring him,
> Fill Thou, O Fire by night
> His soul with store of light!

> "In cold and ice and death,
> O keep his spirit stanch

To Thee, reveal his branch
Of palm, his martyr's wreath.

"Fill Thou his soul with loathing
O kill his one desire
To don their damned clothing,
To warm him at their fire.

"Christ, ere his courage die,
Christ, ere his faith be done
O hearken to my cry
And slay my only son!"

And, now the martyr's song arose, a wraith
Uplifted on the wings of Love and Faith —
"Since we were forty numbered to the race,
Entreat Thee, Lord, deign there be forty crowned!"
"Since by a fast of forty nights and days,
Beseeching God, Elias sought and found
The Beatific Vision. Since Thou hast
Made this same number sacred by Thy fast,
To be henceforth a law of God to man,
Since we were forty numbered to the race
And, since for Thee, O Christ that race began,
Entreat Thee, Lord, by the Centurion's wound,
Entreat Thee, Lord, deign there by forty crowned!"
The Roman slept. Alone, one sentinel,
The fountains of whose heart, perturbed and swayed
By the unconquered psalm that rose and fell
From the one harp of many martyrs made
Sank as he gazed on men so clove asunder,
So blind and deaf and dumb with drouth and cold,
Sank down again in quiet depths of wonder
That men so beaten had one fortress-hold,
One peaceful garden-place remote from fear

Where they could enter in and speak with gods
Or drinking of some Lethe drowsing there
Forget the wine that ran from Roman rods.
Still gazing on the forty martyrs drowned
In a deep tide of prayer his spirit strave

To enter in, it might be and profound,
He saw one of the men whose soul could brave
The bite of cold no more leap off the lake
And plunge into the Thermae craved so long,
And he was sorry for the martyrs' sake
And he remembered then the martyr's song.
And he, Sempronius sent forth his cry
"I am a Christian." As it smote the dark
The guard awoke and he laid slowly by
His armour and stood there before them, stark
And white and beautiful as Adam stood
When God created him in Paradise.

And now the guard held still and rubbed their eyes
And clung together, as a pack of wolves
Threatens a hind with fangs and frenzied cries
Afraid to close; or as a cloud dissolves
Before the sun, they shrank before the glow
Of his abandoned armour and the light
Of nakedness more blinding than the snow
And none laid hands upon the Roman knight
Who made across the ice, and kneeling down,
Laid bare the dark foundations of his soul,
"I fain would have thee wear the martyr's crown,"
The eldest made reply, "and win the goal
We rest are nearing fast, but Christ the Lord
Gave order that His neophytes should be
Baptized both by water and the Word;
And here is naught but ice. No fire have we
To melt a morsel. All our men are cold
As ice itself, and even Melithon
Is cold as they." Sempronius then, "Behold
The tears of one whose soul would enter on
The road you tread unfaltering and gay,
If heathen tears can cleanse the rust of sin
And wash the taint of heathenesse away,
Accept my tears and number me within
The number of the forty." It was done.
And then (as if his hallowing had driven
Forth from the soul of the centurion

A fiend, who, after having vainly striven
To storm the soul of every Roman guard —
Beat back from each obsessèd citadel,
Flung once for all from Heaven and debarred
The hope of taking sanctuary in hell—
Had vowed to wreak revenge upon the Power
Which had so thrust him forth) an impulse drave
The Legion to the lake, and as a Mower,
Ere he scythe down a green withstanding wave
Will, with his blade first lay it low, some fell
Upon Sempronius the centurion,
And slew him where he knelt, and then pell-mell
Began to vent their stifled fury on
The one who had beguiled him to forswear
The Roman eagles and the faith of Rome,
And doing off his girdle and his spear
Had forced a Roman citizen to come
And pay allegiance to a crucified! ...
They broke the Christian magus, limb by limb,
But all their breaking could not break his pride.
They could not crucify the martyrs' hymn.
A million blasphemies rose and died
Like spume before the radiance of the psalm
The dying sang. Each spirit of the dead,
Now free to share the Vision, bear the Palm
Inspired the ruined shell it else had fled
And thrilled it back to life and youth again.
The sun arose. The Legion, half awake,
Began to fling the bodies of the men
On to a hurried fire lit near the lake;
Then, tiring of the carrion, slept again.
And Melithon's mother now forsook the reed
And sought and found the body of her son,
And, hardening the heart she might not heed
Until the deed she had to do was done.
She drew his body gently from the mire,
And, gathering him alive into her lap,
She cast him, still alive, into the fire.

Vision

Upon the charger of my soul,
I rode into a land of dreams;
And, clear above the far-off roll
And plaint of hidden streams,

Imperious and yet forlorn,
Came through the silence of the trees,
The echoes of a golden horn
Calling to distances.

The shadow of the moon had made
The high road of my enterprise;
The solitude held me afraid
Of Hand — of Things — with eyes.

Until the lightning of a hope,
The starshine of a heavenly grail,
Shone o'er the pale untrodden slope,
Gleamed on my shadowy trail.

The Ballad of the Sword

There was a prince of Mawnan went
      In emerald and vair,
      His eyes were blue and innocent,
And he had raven hair.

His body was so shining strong,
So strong as giants be,
The broadswords did to him belong
He brake across his knee.

"Fet me a sword, my armourer,
Shall cleave a knight in twain,
A curvèd sword from Toledo,
The city of the plain."

She's curvèd like a paynim junk,
She's lithe as a hazel wand,
Her brave blade to her hilt had drunk
The life-blood of a land.

She'll cleave an armoured man in twain
From his feather till his spur;
She'll cleave a cobweb on the gorse
And your spider shall not stir.

She is his love and his delight,
She is his staff and rod,
She is his page, she is his knight,
His mother and his god.

O she's a proud, a royal sword.
She's a sword as I avize,
Was sister to the sword that drave
Adam from Paradise!

There was no woman in the world
That mote with her compare,
The morning that the prince unsheathed,
Her body to the air.

"Fet me a priest, Squire Armourer,
And thou shall knighted be,
Forby he be a priest content
To mate my sword an' me.

He's sought to Praze, he sought to Zell
And Zennor, by the sea;
But there's never a priest in all Cornouaille
May dare such deviltry.

And he was out of heart and whisht,
And he was saddle-sore,
Or ever he lit on a stone-blind priest
Lay stagged on Bodmin Moor.

He's hoven him like a barley sack
Until his saddle-bow.
A streak of lightning slit the black
As they rode in Truro.

And Mawnan Church was dizened out
As it were Lammastide,
The people stood as thick as corn,
To gape upon the bride.

Four pages, silked in green and gold,
Held up the canopy,
And Mawnan, loverly, did hold
The sword of sorcery.

The priest heard Mawnan's vow unmoved,
His heart came to a stand
When the Bride made vow in Mawnan's voice,
And her hand was Mawnan's hand.

Though end is made of festival,
Mawnan must now essay
The paramount adventure shall
Jewel his wedding day.

The wedding guests lit Mawnan in,
Gay-hearted, eager-eyed.
The bridesman closed the bridal door
But, alack! and woe betide!

They bare them forth at break of day,
The bridegroom and the bride.
The bride still clasped upon the breast
Her bridal kiss had dyed.

Edward The Seventh

The King, whose urgent hand was yare to sway
To other harmony, the first, faint bars
Awakening on the sullen drums of Mars;
The king, whose words were very gods to stay
The tramp of Europe to the red affray,
The loosing of a myriad scimitars,
Under the quietness of all the stars,
To hush of other music treads his way.

And envoys from a broken universe,
About his peacefulness no leaves shall strow:
No coronals delay upon his herse,
Unto him, dead, no other branches bring
Save of the olive, held unfading now,
Within the quiet fingers of a king.

Nocturn

Midnight. The hour they tap my window-pane,
Thence, without leave, come in, climb on my bed
And into it, entreating to be read –
Newman, Aquinas, Shakespeare and Montaigne:
"Only this one last night, only one page again;
The shortest phrase will ease your aching head,
Chaste as ice, torrid as molten lead.
Fly then to the Olympus where we reign.
There dwells no need of sleep or soup or toil.
There roses bloom for ever, words have wings,
And no harmonious blacksmith swings
A preternaturally brawny arm
Upon an anvil oozing midnight oil."

The Fish Death

I fell . . .
I fell where fishes of the sea,
The fangéd fishes of the sea,
A rainbow, buoyant, devilish,
Swam round in horrid ropes of glee.
In such close coils of fish they clang,
So close they clang they seemed they were
One only Fish, one only Fang.
But had you felt those fleshy eyes,
Those eyes of flesh come crawling through,
Like living bulbs of scorn or shame,
Like living lusts unsatisfied,
You must have anguished to retain
The first intolerable pain,
Filling each nerve, each frantic hair,
With a fierce frenzy of desire
To change to frozen sea or air
Or, in a stream of red-hot hail,
To fuse existence into fire.

(from *Simon Dean and other poems*, 1913)

The Bed
(*from De Hérédia – Le Lit*)

Hung though it be with linen or brocade,
Sad as a tomb or joyful as a nest,
Here man is born, is mated, here finds rest,
Babe, husband, grandsire, grandam, wife or maid.
Be it for burial or bridal sprayed,
Under black crucifix or palm-leaves blest,
From the first dawn till the death-candle drest,
Here all things have beginning, all things fade.

Strait, homely, shuttered, flaunting a pavilion
Triumphant in gold leaf and in vermilion,
Hewn of brute oak, cypress or sycamore –
Happy who sleeps without remorse or dread
In the ancestral bed, immense and hoar,
Where all his folk are born, where all lie dead.

(first published in *Simon Dean and other poems*, 1913)

The Bed
(*from De Hérédia – Le Lit*)

Hung though it be with linen or brocade,
Sad as a tomb or joyful as a nest,
Here man is born, is mated, here finds rest,
Babe, husband, grandsire, grandam, wife or maid.
Be it for burial or bridal sprayed,
Under black crucifix or palm-leaves blest,
From the first dawn till the death-candle drest,
Here all things have beginning, all things fade.

Strait, homely, shuttered, flaunting a pavilion
Triumphant in gold leaf and in vermilion,
Hewn of brute oak, cypress or sycamore –
Happy who sleeps without remorse or dread
In the ancestral bed, immense and hoar,
Where all his fold are born, where all lie dead.

(first published in *Simon Dean and other poems*, 1913)

Noel (I)

God save you all this Christmas Night,
Let nothing you dismay,
For, say – if He'd preferred the light
Of Heaven to lantern ray,
The Sanctus of His Seraph choir
To shepherd-pipe and donkey-bray,
Would you and I be on our way
Home from His Mass to food and fire
This Christmas Day?

Noel (II)

Dark is heaven, white the world:
You bells, ring gaily out!
Jesus is born: the Virgin stoops
To him her charming face.

No festooned curtains are
To shield the Babe from cold:
Nothing but cobwebs hang
From the roof-rafters down.

Atremble on fresh straw
Jesus, this dear small babe;
To warm him in his crib
Donkey and ox breathe down.

Snow-fringes on the barn:
But, overhead, the skies
Are opening; the choir
Of angels all in white
Sing to the hinds, 'Noel!'

(first published in the *Graham Street Quarterly*, winter 1938–39)

Cradle Song

For all the slave-boys diamonds can buy,
So as I have my babe, sire, what care I?'

So string your bosom-harps, mend your aged vair,
Think you I'd rive of Him the leastest hair?

So be there but a breast to sleep my son,
Why tempt Him lie on sofas golden-spun?

Shall I tag cherries, sip your velvet wine,
When as I have His lips, His heart on mine?

Our Lady Mary

Mother of God, Mother of every man,
Grant us to know you as you only can,
Grant us to love you, God's predestined maid,
To whom Archangel Gabriel, kneeling, prayed;
Grant us to serve you as you, smiling, ran
To do the bidding of your mother, Anne.
Offer these prayers to the God-babe you laid
On the proud straw where His new life began.

Our Lady (I)

How dare I, Mother, tombed alive in things
Of earth, approach the kingdom where you reign?
Would I could stumbling follow in your train
Of hurrying shepherds, travel-wearied kings,
And hear the voice they heard; on heaven-bound wings
Ascend to find the Mother I in vain
Pursue so blindly, time and time again,
Until the bell of my last Ave rings.

Mother, forgive the envy of a priest
Abashed to watch a ragged wastrel kneel
At prayer before your shrine, his eyes tear-bright
At seeing one I cannot − never least
Doubt or misgiving checking his appeal
To you, so dim to heart and thought and sight.

Our Lady (II)

How comes this rascal weep before a shrine
Hung with electric-blue, peacock-blue rug,
Blue agapanthus in a lustre jug?
How can an image false in form and line
Evoke for him the Mother-Maid Divine?
What spell has it to mesmerise, be-drug
His sense of beauty, make him long to hug
This image to his heart? See the knave twine
A wilting wreath of buttercups and daisies
Around her pointed feet, watch while he gazes
At her starred crown, orb, diamonded stoles,
Seven silver-paper rapiers thrust
Seven silver-paper buttonholes
On her elaborated bust!

Christmas Night

Acclaim the night! Acclaim the Holy Night
Whose darkest hour held a secret glow
Brighter than any noon Archangels know!
When God for us put off the form of God,
And for our solace chose
A Mother's heart, a breast
At one with his.

Cities of old, in storied ruin sleeping,
Rivers whose beds are rail-roads of today,
Do homage to the Babe the worlds forget:
O Peoples, nations, languages, return
And kiss the feet of Him the stars obey.

Epiphany

Three kings of old in a magnificence
Of samite, silver harness, rubies, fur,
Ride up with gold and frankincense and myrrh
To lay before the Prince of Bethlehem.
No dread have they of Herod in pursuit;
No wastes of sand to travel; never more
will they turn bridle-rein to rest
In their far-off palm-tree'd palaces of Shem ...

Hail, Magi of the East! Hail, Heavened ones!
Free from the tyranny of space and time,
Hear the gay music of our sacring bells
And, leaning over hollies weighed with rime,
Embrace our waxen Christus on your Feast
Of faith made visible − of hope new-sprung
From fading Christmas roses, love new-born
Upon one tumbled stook of Christmas corn.

The Fourth Magus

Again I dream ... A laden caravan,
A fourth wise man, slaves, camels from Lahore,
Take on consistency and bow before
The snow-swept threshold of the lighted khan
Where Joseph, Mary, Jesus God-and-Man,
Gaze up in wonderment as ever more
And more black slaves unroll chameleon store
Of carpets − rugs from Ur and Teheran.

The Magus, silent, robed in royal fur,
Aloof in shadow, musing, eyes the three:
"What jewels will the Heavenly Babe delight?
Which carpet will the Heavenly Babe agree?
My azure, topaz, beryl, emerald, white ...
What can he ask − gold, frankincense or myrrh?"

All Sinners' Day

All Saints who here have for one instant been
Impure, ungrateful, cruel, lazy, mean,
Mary of Magdala, Augustine, Paul,
Pray for me at All Sinners' festival;
Me, with my wings torn from me, a mere moth,
An earthworm trembling in a starling's beak;
Cast but one glance on Him who, for us both,
Blood-ransom paid for gluttony and sloth,
From His death-tree blasted the tree of pride.
And you, my patrons, Thaddeus and Jude,
Patrons of hopes forlorn, crusades fore-doomed,
Embrace one more your broken-hearted son
Fallen at the crucifix beside his bed,
Sleepless and haunted by the vagrant thoughts
Which, like a cloudburst, break about his head
And, foul or holy, soon or late, are bound
To crush the door of his unstable soul;
To you he prays, who through like stress prevailed.

Resurrexit Sicut Dixit
(*or Descendit ad Inferos*)

In Limbo now the spirits of the just,
A field of wild flowers rising out of dust,
A frozen river running free and strong,
Surge round him, speechless in rejoicing trust,
Knowing that He is come for Whom they long,
The Ransomer from Satan, death and lust.

So from a realm unknowing
Of earthly space and time,
Jesus as lightning came:
So from the murky dark
Where once His body, cold
As His death-stone, had laid,
Jesus, our Dawn, arose
To April winds astir
In Judas-tree and lime.

Corpus Domini

At every doorway of the rose-hung street,
On the stone stair-heads, in the angled shade,
Peasants in old-time festival brocade
Took refuge from the unrelenting heat;
These, all by some Mystery made one
With those who dozed or whispered, kissed or played
As silver trumpets rang through the arcade,
Leaned to the far-off sound like wind-blown wheat.

A dark-haired boy, sandalled and naked save
A shift of camel's hair, came first as John
The Baptist: in his wake a yearling lamb,
A crucifix, blest incense; next, a score
Of sunburnt singing-boys in lawn and black
Swept gaily on before a company
Of girls in long lace bridal veils and wreaths
Of oleander, telling rosaries,
But none so fervid that she failed to screen
The lighted taper in her small brown hand
Lest any love-lorn breeze mistake and woo
Its flame for some gold flower.

A group of children who from ribboned frails
Unendingly were flinging to the Host
Flowers of genista, poppy, myrtle, bay;
At last, as from a mist of frankincense
And candle-light and waving cypress boughs,
A priest in silver vestments flowered with gold
To which, as by a spell, his eyes were held;
He gazed, as if these transitory things
Were with the earth, all they had been before
They were created; as if our life were but
A greying garland doomed to pass away.

To him, within the pale orb of the Host,
All he had ever dreaded or desired,
Truth, wisdom, power, peace and righteousness,
As in a crystal mirror, stood revealed,

And so, adoring his uplifted God,
Wonder, profoundest wonder filled his soul.

This Host he held before him was, he knew,
But one of thousands he, with Christ's last words,
Had blessed and raised to God at break of dawn;
As known to him, as dearly natural
As his young olive trees, his violin,
The cedar press where lay the folded alb
He would at death be clothed in, the pale crown
Of 'everlastings' on his mother's grave.

This Host was close to these persisting things.
In this, then, dwelt the marvel; here abode
The Lord who made the beauty of the world,
The sun, the moon, and all the stars that be,
The solace and the menace of the sea.

Came holding, shaded by a baldaquin
Of white and silver tissue, thin with age,
A golden monstrance like an outspread fan,

I Leaned Upon The Beauty of the World
(*"Je m'appuyai sur la beauté du monde."*)

I leaned upon the beauty of the world,
From winter suns I drank the blood-red wine,
And from the diamond nights I stole
The mornings pearled; May for me alone,
Swfit to my bidding, first for me unfurled
Her cool green flame – the frail, chaste, shy fanfare
Of every hart's-tongue, every maidenhair.
I should have been transfixed with happiness
For all these favours, yet, despite them all,
The heavens of my soul were overcast,
The eagles of my soul unsatisfied,
Until above the altar of the sea,
Beyond the lighted candles of the stars,
I saw God elevate His Host, the moon.

N.B. I stole the first line and the first line only from M. Audiguer while travelling in train to Rome. The poem was in a magazine, *Je Sais Tout*. –
L.S.W.

Travail

...Tensely as he, who, burdened with the Host,
Through a long night of storm, at each fresh gust
Crams down his cap securely, draws his cloak
More straitly round him steadily as he
Wrestles the frenzied wind, out of the moor,
Halts to take breath at the wide-open door,
Enters the house with Christ, lays down the pyx
On the rough altar near the crucifix.

O, would my heart beat as a heart like this,
For then, by some strange unimagined force –
No sudden inflow of supernal strength,
No miracle creating me
Sultan of Time and Space, but by a power
Released from him who bore the muffled Host,
I would fling wide the arms of my enamoured soul
And gather in one fond embrace the Whole ...

The Tabernacle in Wartime

The Holy Hour was over — it was cold!
The Home of God seemed a forsaken Home.
The spark that swayed before the hidden Host,
The tapers cowering before the Rood,
Were fires lit and tended by themselves.
A stillness reigns where never a sound comes.
The only stir in that withdrawn Dominion,
The only music borne upon the air
In the whiteness of a sea of upturned faces,
The phantom, far-off drone of engines' thrums.

Old France

'*Credo in unum Deum*' – the same tones
Reverberating on the granite stones
Which for a thousand years had drunk the words
Known to Celts, Greeks, Icelanders, Turks and Kurds.
Outside, the ceaseless praise of twittering birds.
Inside the church, a group of kerchiefed crones,
Each jealousing the market frail she owns,
Fruit, eggs, vegetables and chickens – mostly bones.
The bowed heads of men, lit by the slanting sun.
Hear them echo, softly, '*Credo in unum Deum*'.

The beauty of the France I knew of old ...
My memories brighten as the years unfold ...

Horizon

Like phantom ships on the horizon-line
My thoughts escape; escaping, challenge me
To draw them back again across the sea –
And softly, suddenly, as from a shrine,
A voice, my own and yet not wholly mine,
Is whispering from where the phantoms be,
'We are no longer yours, but broken free
To wander where we will. Your christening wine,
The wild imaginary names you gave,
Are unremembered as a passing wave;
Regard us not as puppets you can fill
With power to dance and posture at your will,
But Frankensteins aris'n to haunt your bed,
And lay you out, and watch you lying dead.'

Pot Pourri

Who would a royal wine outpour
In darkened or ignoble glass?
Let us be resolute to hoard
The minutes of a summer hour
In radiant unaccustomed urns
Created of the very light
They were predestinate to hold;
And when the winter hours return
And we are desolate withal —
For faces at the emptied hearth
Are countenances of the dead —
Let us unseal, with reverent haste,
Those urns of glory and of light,
To breathe the sacred fragrances
Of roses from forgotten bowers,
Of rivers whose remembered banks
Are filled again with irises,

(From *Simon Dean and Other Poems*, 1913)

Storm on the Veldt

Already, while the storm was pondering
Whether or no to break upon the veldt,
The birded palms, asleep like harvesters
Rid of their last vast load and now, foreknowing
The doom to come, stiffen from wood to steel,
And, at the seldom sign so dire with omen,
Lions and zebra, jackals, gnus, gazelles
Huddle together, fear-transformed
To beasts of an old fabliau: as the last
Lame zebra loped to windward of the blast,
Rain as of melting stalactites roared down.

Anniversary of Confirmation

O God, whose lightnings in their flash reveal
The secrets of the soul, dissolve the dense
Miasmas of the prison-house of sense,
And scourge; and, scourging, curb and bring to
   heel
The chargers of our pride and bastard zeal,
Hear, as he eats the bread of penitence
In bitterness of soul, a soul's appeal
To you, his first love and his one ideal:
Whisper my spirit in the far-off voice
First heard when I to your encounters rode;
Emblaze upon the armour once I wore
The cross of boyhood's free and selfless choice;
To your apostate liegeman, Lord, restore
The stainless Knighthood first your love bestowed.

The General Judgement

When Earth is in her death-throes, when the last
Of her last days is numbered, the plied skein
Of her four Seasons ravelled, riven in twain,
The Avenue of the Years laid low and cast
Adrift upon the river of the past,
And seed and harvest, frost and summer rain
Are garments she will never wear again –
I, even I shall hear the Judgement-blast,
And, prostrate in that hour of awe, look up
To Him whom I abandoned, veil my eyes
Before the searching light of that fell Sign
Whereon I crucified Him – Man Divine,
The Slave who drained for me the poison-cup
Of one and all my dark iniquities.

All Soul's Day, Gunwalloe (1913)

Unto what tryst, what mermaid sarabands,
Are you, white-robed children, dancing, bound,
Chrysanthemums of orange flashed with gold
And candles of dull topaz in your hands?
By what sea-god's importunate demands
In wind-waved robes of faded purple gowned,
By whose black-magic forcibly patrolled,
Bearing funebrial torches o'er the sands?

'Tis for no dancing, this our fine array.
The frankincense, the flowers we seaward fling
Are to no Neptune flung: for him we sound
No music magical this All Souls' Day
In our atonement, our peace-offering
Devoted by the living to the drowned.

"Ecoute. Quelqu'un Chante ..."
(*translated from a poem by Charles Guerin*)

Come hearken, Poet; someone sighs or sings a strain,
But gay or sad no man can tell,
And may your eager pen arouse from sleep
Your age-embalméd soul to catch the music of that secret
voice.
Listen with more than miser's care today
For the Divine Companion who to you
Unveils your hidden soul. Tomorrow, e'er
Dawn fires the sky he will have flown,
For no man ever yet saw
The same fire glow,
Or the first love offered to his youth,
Arise to life once more.

"Eheu! Fugaces, Postume ..."
(Horace's Odes, Book 2, 14:
"Alas, Posthumus, the flying years glide by
And are lost to me ...")

The children I once sat upon my knee
Have all grown far away from me ...
Alas! My salad says.
Watch as I watched them (gardening) plundering my
   maize.
At eager football, watch them as they pile
One on another in a mudden'd scrum,
Blooded all over – paws and ears and bum.
Or at our baths, a silvery shoal of fish
Dive without splashing for the prize Form-dish.
Alas, the long, fond, farewell embraces
(Aheu! Fugaces ....)
The winner of this noble loving-cup,
Plucking his courage and his silk slip up,
Tongue-tied, tight-lipped, received it from the Dame.
O. proudly shy was he to hear his name!

The Prior

At Pentecost, which fell that year in June,
When from a night of dreams the prior woke,
He knew himself delivered from the yoke
Of wickedness, and in exulting tune
With the Fire Feast of God the One-Triune.
Far from his cell above a Spanish oak
He was aware of voices — fisher-folk
Entreating God for him above the dune.
The prison-pit where late he had been thrust
Now, with his dreams, was gone; now, like a bird
Escaped unwounded from the fowler's snare,
He can ascend to God undeterred
By idle fears, to His loved hands entrust
His sorriest, weakest, driest flower of prayer.

The Sacred Heart (I)

"His Sacred Heart
No symbol is,
No phantasy."

"Apart, remote
From any griefs
Or joys of ours?"

"No; for It draws
All souls who will
Into Its peace.

At that pure Source,
By that bright Stream,
Man lays his load,
Man dreams his dream.

In that great Room
Takes shelter, bares
His every wound;
Till, with flung arms,
Christ comes to him."

The Sacred Heart (II)

The Sacred Heart no phantom is
Nor phantasy.
By that bright Source man lays his load,
In that vast Room finds refuge there,
In calm may feast,
Till with flung arms the Christ draws nigh."

This was Father Wason's last poem, dictated by him on the Feast of the
Sacred Heart, 16th June, 1950, Limehouse.

The Anglican Alphabet

A is the Anglican brimfull of gas,
B is for breakfast he eats before mass,
C are the Curates at Cuddesdon bred,
D are the Districts, Perambu*lated*,
E is the Eagle, sublimely absurd,
F are the females that polish that bird,
G is the Guild of the Church Lads Brigade,
H is the helluva row that they made,
I is the incense we "can't see our way too",
J is St Joseph they won't let us pray to,
K is the Key to the Vicar's position,
L is the lace that we wear at the Misson,
M is the Mattins we have at eleven
N is the nonsense we talk about heaven,
O is the Octave we keep up with preaching,
P is the Prayer Book "our Standard of Teaching",
Q is the Choir of Communicant Laymen,
R is the roar of the "Seven-fold Amen",
S is the stole all embroidered with lotuses,
T is the tone for giving out notices,
U is the "Use" that we have from our "Aunt"
V is the Vicar who says "No you Can't",
W is the wife whom our Vicar has wed,
X is the u*x*orious life that they've led!

(attributed to the Revd. Sandys Wason, Vicar of Cury with Gunwalloe
c.1905)

Binns

A green perambulator
   A brace of placid twins,
The man an aviator,
   By name Augustus Binns.

The woman's name Augusta,
   A working-woman she,
Employed upon Lincrusta,
   At Birchington-on-sea.

She wore a sprig of gentian,
   Stuck in her purple blouse,
A flower I may perhaps mention
   Grew on the Binns' house.

She had another, scarlet,
   With white forget-me-nots.
Her seamstress called it "Star-lit";
   Her rivals called it "Spots."

Her *garde-robe* was extensive,
   But, as she truly said:-
"I bought them with the pence I've
   Economized on bread."

Her form was round and hearty!
   Her smile serene, yet fond,
     The mien of an Astarte,
   The colouring of a blonde.

Augustus, not so handsome
   Had hair as exquisite.
     Exposure on the Rand, some
Declared, had turned it white.

His beard was vaguely auburn;
   He'd grown it to obscure
A nasty-looking, raw burn
   No specialist could cure.

It was a standing scandal
  Until he grew a beard,
A vegetable handle,
  To which the twins adhered.

To come back to his visage,
  Three verses higher up,
Augustus carried his age
  As topers carry Cup.

His features had the far-away
  Expression they reveal
Who from a cake of caraway
  Divert the candied peel.

They lived in Bina Cottage
  In Cleopatra Street.
The twins grew up on pottage!
  They lived on butcher's meat.

The small boy's name was 'Zekiel,
  The small girl's name was Flo'.
I've told the beginning; the sequel
  I now proceed to show.

The vehicle was standing
  Outside the private door
Of a public-house demanding
  A word or two or more.

It was called "the Pig in clover."
  Its landlord's name was Jones;
Its balcony looked over
  A shop for rags and bones.

It leaned on a reputation
  For purity of beer;
It was opposite the station.
  A minute from the pier.

The vehicle was waiting
  Upon the curb outside.
The twins began debating;
  The pram began to slide.

It slid along the pavement,
  Slid like a clock-work toy,
Slid to the watery grave, meant
  To hold the girl and boy.

Flashed like a picture post-card
  Flashes from over-seas,
Till a present-minded coastguard
  Caught it between his knees.

He caught it twirling, sinking
  And swirling in the flood;
He caught it up like winking,
  And wiped away the mud.

He wiped the infants' faces,
  He wiped their robes and hair.
The infants made grimaces;
  The coastguard spoke them fair.

He spoke them fair and freely,
  Did that coastguard celibate.
He offered them a mealy
  Potato on a plate.

Now while this baby-feeding
  Or infant hunger-strike
Was quietly proceeding
  Or loudly, if you like,

Unconscious of the dipping
  The infant Binns had had,
The parent Binns were sipping
  A glass of something glad.

A glass of something gladsome,
  Two hot unsweetened gins;
The beverage had had some
  Effect upon the Binns.

Their faces had the glamour,
  That flush of crimson lake
Remarked on the plum jam our
  Grand-parents used to make.

The Binns had turned the corner
  Dividing rest from sloth,
And Time the old suborner
  Who preys upon our youth

Had with his fell mandragora
  Beguiled them to forget
That over Life's Niagara,
  There is a sun . . . to set.

Meanwhile the coastguard, Davis,
  Embarrassed how to treat
The whimsies of the babies
  Had wheeled them up the street

To where a printed notice,
  "Police," confronted one
(The P in myosotis
  The smaller lettering, dun.)

A constable in mufti
  Perused the local paper;
His buff suit and his buff tie
  Came from the local draper.

He heard the whole recital,
  He took a note or two,
"I think, Sam, if that's quite all
  There's one thing you might do.

"The Home for Waifs and Strays is
  Or seems to be, the place.
They take in urgent cases;
  This is an urgent case.

"The babes are clearly dirty;
  They both require a snack;
The Waifs tea at four-thirty,
  Our tea-hour's been put back."

Now, though the morning mavises
  Which woke the Waifs and Strays
Awoke the house next Davis'
  With matutinal lays;

Although the residences
  Lay almost cheek by jowl
And parallel pine fences
  Enclosed collateral fowl,

To put the thing concisely
  He did *not* care to wheel
The pram however nicely
  To fresh courts of appeal.

And as he hesitated,
  He heard a train-bell ring,
His course was adumbrated —
  "The station is the thing!"

He ran them down the platform,
  He dumped them from the pram,
He set them on the flat form,
  As one might set a ham.

He had the vehicle labelled
  The first name that occurred;
The infants he enabled
  Into a crowded third.

And then, to calm the tension
He felt pervading there,
He flung a "Let me mention
The missus will be here

"In almost half a second;
She's taking tickets now."
And violently beckoned,
And then ... he made his bow.

From *Magenta Minutes* Nonsense Verses by Sandys Wason. (Published.
Lond, Max Goschen, Ltd. 1913)

Fir-Cones

Like open fir-cones dipped in fire and cream
the thunder clouds were piling up the sky;
and from the sea, a wing of them leapt high
above the hills; the prow of a trireme
drifting on breakers to the smoky gleam
of torches lifted, every torch an eye,
fixed on the fall and rising of her beam.

While from the cliffs, a snake of women garbed
in long white robes, with floating flaxen hair
and bows of cedar-wood and arrows barbed
in single file crawled down the granite stair.

(The first two lines are from 'Armed with madness' by Mary Butts)

Love

There sate a muffin, tinged with pink
   Upon a kind of form it brought,
And thought of nothing; only think
   What nothing means to men of thought.

A crumpet chanced to pass that way;
   It came on from a dancing-tea.
It took a taxi; crumpets may
   Take taxi-cabs without a fee.

The muffin blushed; when muffins blush
   It never, never does to sneeze.
It came with what is called a rush.
   A tiger-skin lay on its knees.

'What ails the babe?' The muffin said,
   And stroked her long magnetic ear.
'I'll lead you to the strawberry bed:
   It used to be a belvedere'.

The crumpet stopped a long long stop
   Beyond the edge of earthly things
To teach a stranded acid-drop
   To dredge for shuttle-cocks in swings.

He was a subtler, saner thing,
   A thing between the then and now,
As certain as the days of spring,
   As unpretending as a sough.

It could not speak below its throat,
   Its eyelashes prevented that.
It wore a purple petticoat,
   It wore a picture post-card hat.

She led the way the crumpet took
   Across the lotus of the land.
The dedication of a book
   One finds in an umbrella-stand

Was nothing to the girlish smile,
   Was nothing to the summer laugh
With which she lightened mile on mile
   Of unexasperating chaff.

The voice within the tears of love,
   The amber in the fly's embrace,
Were buttoned tightly in the glove
   Of absolutely perfect grace.

She had that wayworn, wriggling air,
   Sly, sub-terrene and yet opaque,
Which goes with bright horse-chestnut hair
   And fascinates the rattlesnake.

He was a subtler, saner thing
   A thing between the then and now,
As certain as the days of spring,
   As unpretending as a slough.

A glimmering of something gone,
   An anguish or at most a word,
The serious perhaps alone
   Re-ember from the harpsichord,

Grew in between the two who ran
   So patiently, so tuned and blithe
To where the God forgets the man
   And where the grass, alas! The scythe.

It grew, a world of moods apart,
   A trail of semi-tones unheard
To sound the beatings of a heart
   With glamours of a hope deferred.

Until across the awn and spathe
   And moil and spilth of old romance
They lay upon the inmost lathe
   Of undetermined circumstance.

Ars Poetica (I)

I, in writing mood, sate me down under a quince tree,
Keyed up for the thousandth time to evolve
The poem of a life-time, a poem in the grand manner,
There lay the snag of verse-making, *saleable* verses.
Editors were prone to look down their noses
At my persevering attempts
To get, so to speak, right down into the tautest filaments
Of Dryden's sub-consciousness, disentangling & washing
    & brushing-up
Some posthumous pearl of his, overlooked by the most
    inquisitive
Of his biographers.
And then a quince fell from the tree i was sitting under
And i saw in a flash where i had gone utterly wrong:
The thing to do and i was the man to do the thing
Was not so much the elimination of the un-essential
As to get down, in comfortable dust-proof over-alls,
To bed-rock.
Coming to grips with the basic adamantine quintessence
    of verse,
Words of one or (sometimes) two syllables:
For what, after all, was poetry made of?
Not of things to eat or drink or be merry with,
However yare or buxom or mouth-worthy,
Not of ediments, elements and merriments, as i hinted a
    line or two above,
But of words to be found in the commonest dictionaries
    of mankind.

Adolphus

Here lieth one whose early days were spent
On ladders listening, dreaming, scheming; an
Enthusiastic, auburn-haired young man:
The nordic Wilberforce whom Nietzsche sent
To free the slaves of Europe, circumvent
The Chamberlain of Mars and draft a plan
To neutralize, evacuate or ban
The sleepless spectre of encirclement.

Parnassus or Valhalla? Both, he thought
Had Liebensraum for gods of sword and pen;
Parnassus dealt exclusively in odes,
Valhalla built its halls for gods, not men.
Alas! Adolphus wanders sombre-eyed,
His *Doppelganger* draggling by his side.

Accredited the Nobel prize for peace
For forwarding the libraries of Greece
A clear synopsis of his new "Mein Kampf",
Adolphus, tired but heartened on the whole,
Succumbs, alas! to chronic writers' cramp
And Clio to Parnassus wafts his soul.

(Only young readers will need to be told that this poem refers to Herr
Hitler).

Evacuees at Oxford, "Hitler's War"

Sleeping in the Hall, sleeping in the House,
Unperturbed by Wolsey, Thomas Strong and Rowse
Sleeping the Hall, snug as bug or louse.

Lay our refugees, our evacuees
obese Japanese, Chinese, Portuguese,
A very likely centre-piece for fleas.

Waving in the Corn, waving in the quads,
drying on and on, drying oh! ye gods!
strewn about the place where one sat for mods,

Washing hung on lines. "Where oh! where's the police?"
"Refugeeing's right! I have one, a niece,
living as i'm told, near a Wren hospice"

"Sorry if i dropped such a fearsome brick.
Washing everywhere is a Nazi trick
bringing bombs on all and every Benedick.

Town

I met a clergymanly man
   Prostrate in the Strand,
He sucked a brace of oranges;
   One orange in each hand.

He had a gentle racial air,
   He wore the clothes one wears;
The parting of his ample hair
   Had been there thirty years.

He held his cheek up to the sun;
   He let the sunlight fall
Half in contempt and half in fun
   And bitterly withal.

His words were few and special words;
   They calmed the throbs that rose,
Like crumbs one offers to the birds
   Or biscuits to the does.

Before he spoke I realized
   How false conventions are;
I sized him up like one who sized
   A cocktail at a bar.

He spoke in minuets of sound.
   I listened all the while
'Life's little ironies' went round
   The gentlewomen's mile.

It was not that his words were rare
   Or few and far between.
They had the crisp conclusive air
   Of some stray Pleiocene,

Of some vague far-off dim trombone,
   Held lengthwise to the breast,
The rapt reverberate monotone
   Of working-men at rest.

He said: 'I round in scarlet kilts
　　The mulberry-bush of life;
And carves the nightingales of hope
　　With memory's carving-knife.

'I keep my matches in a box,
　　I strike them on the lid,
I climb above the tidal rocks
　　Ahasuerus did.

'I take away the strain of life,
　　I walk away its throes;
O I keep couched within my heart
　　The Romaunt of the Rose!"

'I am a man as men are made;
　　I have the feelings men
Deny or gratify in trade
　　Or chaffer with a pen.

'I kept a shop in Araby,
　　The world was clean and young;
My typist was a Caribee;
　　Obese but over-strung.

'I paid him for the work he did
　　By piece-time or the hour,
The doorway of the shop was hid
　　With pomegranates in flower.

'My customers were Turkish nuns,
　　The novices, Chocktaws;
They lived on septic Sally Lunns.
　　Devoted to the cause'.

And still at every Christmas time
　　I see the old man sit
And suck on at his oranges
　　And sit and sit and sit.

Tiger etc

A tiger unmentioned by Kipling
A tailless and whiskerless stripling
Served all our Low Masses
At St Nicholas's
Till pitched from a dog-cart for tippling.

A rose and cream abbess, Mère Esther
Took a fancy being a Wax Vesta
Struck plumb on the head
Unignited, she bled
Interrupting the barman's siesta.

My aunt knew a man of the world
Whose whiskers and pockets were curled.
Fast girls and slow horses
Were all his resources
When into Eternity hurled.

A lady from Bugthorp, unwed,
Said 'There cannot be fleas in my bed.
The insect you thumb
Is a survivor of some
From a crows nest, R.N. off Spithead'.

A tricksy equestrian queen
Wore a wig hardly fit to be seen,
When this item fell off
Her mount staged a cough
Thus avoiding a hair-raising scene.

A countryman clubman Eugene
Knew Bathsheba, Circe, Undine.
Ticked off by the Secretary! −
'True, I'm a peccatory
But it's willow I wear for you, Jean.'

There once was an orderly parrot
Whose collar was stamped 18 Carat;

When it rained she would perch
On the spire of Bow Church
With her pipe and a bottle of claret.

There once was a town-planning tortoise
'Quelque bruit' in a government caucus;
When Churchill went out
He got lost in a spout
Gushing tears over tenement quarters.

There once was a family bed
With 4 legs and a foot and a head.
There were 24 pillows
By Waring and Gillows
And the man who designed it is dead.

The Hermit

My mind is wandering. It's the pain
I suffer. No one dares
To read me Lorna Doone again
Or buy me William pears.

And though the cave I live in is
As comfy as maybe,
I own I languishingly miss
My old, gold, silk settee.

And since my daily nourishment
Is laver, plain or curried,
My one and only encouragement
Is never to be hurried.

Hurry is ill for man or snail;
It sets the nerves revolving.
The remedy is turning tail
And complex cross-word solving.

Death Has Wings

Here Hell is for the moment stilled. Death here
his wings has now refolded. Fire now
has dimmed her smallest spark, and earth put out
her blazing craters. Strangely I begin
to dream that life is beautiful; believe
in other tidings, mornings, yes, and springs.

In thee, staunch country, I believe; erect
above thy smoking ruins. O thou Land
of Nelson, under mothering stars I hear
recurrent, like a slowly beating heart
the sound of thy *eternal* sea.

(Translated from a French poem published in the Times, written during
an air-raid)

Ou Sont Les Mages D'Antan?

Since Ronsard and Verhaeren (bards of yore)
with other sterling poets dared foretell
that fans of theirs would of an evening spell
over their verse, must i, a troubadour
with sonnets laurelled, myrtled odes galore,
be pilloried if i predict that swell
ladies and gents will phone *mine* from Dingley Dell
to typistes teaing on a Tyneside tor?

will take a glance at the loose-limbed colleens
Polymnia blessed me with? i'm not a person
to think my little family can rival
Ronsard's vast brood. It is for one short verse on
a single row of scarlet runner beans
that i lay claim to ultimate survival.

Some verses for Daisy Deas.

"Boy babies matter very little. It is unnecessary to count
anyone except the girls".
(Sir William Beveridge-on the population question).

The Importance of Being Ernestine

Girls had one use; they ministered to man:
Darned Man's pyjamas, chose higs legs of pork.
Girls' hands were handy though their brains were bran,
Man thought for them, did all the thinking-work.

Man (finding girls had tongues) invented means
To do away with girlies: − telephones,
C.O.D. − shopping, robots, slot-machines
For fish-and-chips, and raisins minus stones.

'A thing Slipp'd Idly From Me'

The open coal-fire's bright unwinking gaze,
The callous chit-chat of my parlour clock,
Remind me of my young impervious days
When first I wrote ballades and roundelays.

The clock wants winding up, the fire is out,
The cat is pining for a midnight stroll,
There's nothing left to drink but bottled stout,
And nothing left to eat but sausage-roll.

La Chanson de Marie-des-Anges

Once on a time, a poor fellow,
   et lon la laire,
   et lon lan la,
once on a time a poor fellow
loved a gal but she said no!

Says she to him: bring, as six do strike,
   et lon la laire,
   et lon lan la,
says she to him; bring as six do strike
your mother's heart for my tyke.

Off goes he and mama to slay,
   et lon la laire,
   et lon lan la,
off goes he, mama to slay,
takes her heart and runs away.

As he runned, down he fell,
   et lon la laire,
   et lon lan la,
as he runned, down he fell,
rolled to earth, heart as well.

And while heart she roll round,
   et lon la laire,
   et lon lan la,
and while heart she roll round,
he heard heart speak from ground.

And says heart, weeping wild,
   et lon la laire,
   et lon lan la,
and says heart, weeping wild,
hurt yourself, pool lil' child?

Jean Richepin.

Kabale Und Liebe

Many a mad magenta minute
Lights the lavender of Life;
Keren-happuch at her spinet,
Psalms the scarlet song of strife.'
Keren-happuch is my wife.

Spinet carving olive stanzas,
   Orange fricassées of sound,
Nicotine extravaganzas,
   Like a cheese at evening found,
   Sitting primrose on the ground.

Spinet, cast thy chiaroscuro
   O'er the omelette of the past;
Drawn from thy enamelled bureau,
   Bind thy night-shirt to the mast,
   Derelict but not outcast.

With a harsh pea-green "Remember"
   From the horoscope of Ruth
Frame the language of December
With the silver-gilt of Truth,
   Consecrated to thy youth.

The first poem in the collection: Magenta Minutes published. 1913 by
Max Goschen, 20 Great Russell Street, WC. by Sandys Wason.

Temptation

How can I, haunted by a host of doubts
of God, eternity, sacrament and creed
consent without demur to intercede
for those who fail to hear the ribald shouts
of demons mocking, see no icy gouts
of sweat pour off me as I come to read
the Canon of the Mass? How can I heed
the woes of others, when, like roundabouts

these vile mistrusts are whirring through my brain
and make me desperate to throw aside
as a vain
fantastic masquerade? Saint Isidor
come to my help; Saint Anthony, implore
for me, so daily tempted, hourly crucified.

The See of T . . .

"O Joseph, go and beat the kettle drum,
  And beat the kettle drum,
  And beat the kettle drum
Across the C of E."
The Western rite was wild and stank of Rome,
  And all alone went he.

The Western rite crept up along the land,
  And o'er and o'er the land,
  And round and round the land,
As far as J could see.
The Eucharist peeped out – that hidden hand –
  And nearer Rome came we.

They put him on a cope out-roming Rome,
  The cruel, fawning Rome,
  The cruel, hungry Rome,
In a nave for all to see.
But still the Prot-men hear his kettle-drum
Across the C of E.

With apologies to the late Charles Kingsley. (This poem refers to the
right Revd Joseph Wellington Hunkin, Bishop of the See of Truro from
1935 to 1951, who relentlessly tried to stamp out Anglo-Catholicism in
his diocese, P.E.B-G).

Index of Poems